BOOTSTRAPPING ETHICS

BOOTSTRAPPING ETHICS

INTEGRITY RISK MANAGEMENT FOR REAL-WORLD APPLICATION

RUPERT EVILL

WILEY

Registered Offices
John Wiley & Sons, Inc., 111 River Street, Hoboken, NJ 07030, USA
John Wiley & Sons Ltd, The Atrium, Southern Gate, Chichester, West Sussex, PO19 8SQ, UK

Editorial Office

The Atrium, Southern Gate, Chichester, West Sussex, PO19 8SQ, UK
For details of our global editorial offices, customer services, and more information about Wiley products visit us at www.wiley.com.

Library of Congress Cataloging-in-Publication Data is Available:

ISBN 9781119874904 (Hardback)
ISBN 9781119874928 (ePDF)
ISBN 9781119874911 (ePub)

Cover Design: Wiley
Cover Image: © Jakub Krechowicz/Shutterstock

Set in 13/16 pt Minion Pro by Straive, Chennai, India
Printed and bound by CPI Group (UK) Ltd, Croydon, CR0 4YY

C9781119874904_280922

CONTENTS

PREFACE

I spent most of my life in the shadows. In 2015, when I met my wife, she did her background check on me and became very concerned. I had no (public) profile, and many questions followed. I'd spent my career in the grey world of risk. I'd been a counter-terrorism analyst (much less glamorous than it sounds), an investigator, an intelligence gatherer, a political risk wonk, a crisis responder, a behavioural analyst, and an integrity risk advisor. I travelled this path by volunteering for every exciting project, job, and opportunity – by taking risks. I am and was happy being the clueless newbie learning from masters. I've been blessed with mentors like Dr Cliff Lansley and Dane Chamorro, who taught me the arts of deception detection and tradecraft. I've also learned from dozens of genius colleagues and clients – too many to mention; the people I still speak to regularly.

In retrospect, and I take no credit for planning this, the path gives me a rounded understanding of risk. Terrorists, corrupt politicians, fraudsters, hackers, harassers, and general baddies are not that different. They're humans; we need to know how the motives, means, and methods differ. Integrity risks – by which I mean most things that cause scandals – are a further unifier. All the baddies want money (or power). Whether you're smuggling ivory, building bombs, stealing state secrets, or ripping off your employer, if we're managing integrity risks, we reduce your chances of success.

I don't see integrity risks as figures – I am numerically useless. I see how caustic and vicious this corruption and abuse of power are. These risks gravely threaten our planet, wildlife, human existence, and hope. If we don't take them seriously, we're in trouble. We do our bit if you and I cut off the funding, increase accountability, and respond honestly to risk. The small bribe you pay isn't a drop in the ocean; as Rumi said, "You are the ocean in a drop."

In 2019, I started Ethics Insight. I was woefully unprepared to be a business owner. I made many mistakes, especially around marketing and sales – two areas I'd barely had to contend with previously. I was bewildered by the options – channels, funnels, adverts, email campaigns, cold leads, warm leads, it was all gibberish. It was a wonderful lesson. Risk had become implicit knowledge to me, just as marketing know-how was for all the people I read and spoke to. I realised why most people didn't understand what I did – I was speaking gibberish.

The pandemic necessitated a massive transformation as my traditional investigative work (and behavioural analysis training gigs) disappeared – 51 investigations in 2019 became three in 2020. A good friend (James Ritchie) told me as I prevaricated about entering the LinkedIn world of self-promotion, public speaking, and authoring, "Get over yourself." So I did. I used my followers and connections as a laboratory – assessing which risk simplification ideas worked (or not). I learned that if risk is ever to be relevant, it must start with more personal and human constructs (our values, ethics, and beliefs).

As I found my voice, the publisher Wiley found me. They asked me to write a book making risk relevant to you, a broader audience.

We all make risk-based decisions daily. We all face integrity and ethical challenges. If you'd like to improve, I hope this book will help you.

I can't and won't cover every facet of risk. You will be disappointed if you're looking for environmental, social, and governance (ESG) risk coverage. Corruption, dishonesty (inauthenticity, if I'm being kind), and abuse of power facilitate most ills ESG is concerned with, but I think ESG in its current form is useless. Not the concept, but the metric-driven performative crap peddled by charlatan advisors and cynical institutions. No one person can cogently explain plastic effluents, noise pollution, indigenous land rights, board composition, reporting best practice and sanctions. Again, I focus on integrity risk as it's the currency in which most organisational ills are transacted. My focus is on the root causes of rot, not treating every risk malaise.

This book will borrow statistics and survey data here and there, but, for better or worse, I based it on my experiences managing thousands of projects in more than 50 countries. I look for patterns, overlap, and consistency. Clarity. Enough gibberish, I hope!

INTRODUCTION

I don't like compliance. The very word is jarring, implying control of someone over another. I remember when I first came across the organisational structure and function of compliance. I have worked in some exciting areas, including crisis response, counter-terrorism, and political risk. I loved that work. I didn't realise it then, but it's all about people and why we do what we do. I moved from that job to one in investigations, which included conducting due diligence on the prospective clients of prominent investment banks. Due diligence – know your customer – is snooping into someone's background. Our job was to ensure the bank wasn't onboarding clients with more skeletons in their closet than a medical training aid factory.

When we delivered our reports, it became apparent that the focus was another acronym: CYA = cover your ass/arse. All too often, organisations term this butt-bashfulness, compliance. I remember sitting on a call with a few bankers and my Russia analyst colleague. We'd found strong evidence that a serving public official almost certainly owned a prospective business they wished to finance through offshore holdings. Officials should not hold non-disclosed commercial interests, generally. The bankers asked if we had documentary proof of the shareholding. The complex owner-ship structure quickly left Russia for sunny offshore jurisdictions with ironclad secrecy. We did not. Our evidence followed testimony from former and existing employees. They confirmed that the official owned the business; he had an office with a dialysis machine (to cleanse his blood of all the cocaine). This official also had significant alcohol and drug abuse issues, which had resulted in his killing or maiming people (multiple occasions) while driving under the influence. The bankers asked us if the deaths had led to prosecutions. We confirmed they had not, as he'd bribed the police and judiciary. They countered by requesting documentary evidence of that bribery (our evidence was circumstantial but corroborated by multiple sources). Obtaining physical proof of corruption is incredibly challenging, as you require access to (often offshore) accounts and surveillance, among other methods. The call concluded with the bankers saying, "Well, then, as we see it, you don't have physical proof of wrongdoing, so I think we can proceed."

Compliance is often obeying clearly defined rules or pretending to. In this example, it is legal if it's not proven criminal. Compliance can be the base level of morality in many situations.

Why, therefore, am I writing a book covering topics that would be classed (by many) as compliance? Because I care about risk, and more specifically, helping people make ethically minded and risk-based decisions. I want to make integrity risk-relevant – all risks an organisation might face with ethical components. This broad church – from corruption to human rights to discrimination – overlaps more than it digresses.

In 1973, Donald R. Cressey devised what is now known as Cressey's Fraud Triangle.[1] Fraud, in this case, is defined so broadly as to cover most crimes that will occur in an organisation. The model posited that fraudulent acts were a function of opportunity, rationalisation, and pressure. Compliance, for many years, focused principally on the opportunity part, where systems and processes do not exist or are insufficient. For example, stealing from the cash register because there is no CCTV monitoring and balance checks are irregular or sloppy. It makes sense to focus on opportunity; it is a variable we (think we) can control.

In my experience over the past 20 (or so) years, an opportunity is seldom the main reason. This hunch is borne out in the survey data that the Association of Certified Fraud Examiners (ACFE) gather yearly in their Report to the Nations.[2] Their report, surveying some of their 90,000 (and growing) members, who are focused on investigations, typically indicates that controls failure is the primary reason for violations in roughly a third of cases.

What's happening in the majority of cases? Well, that would be where pressure and rationalisation come into play. This human element is where I live and work. Pressure is a massive area we will unpack in some detail, but another word for it that may resonate more is *motive*. That's what makes us cut corners, do things we should not, and often compromise our ethics for the benefit of our employer. Understanding why we make the decisions we do and the cultural, situational, and psychological reasons for ethical and compliance failures is, I believe, the key to better organisational ethics and behaviour.

It is that mission that keeps me motivated. Why? Because I've spent most of my career working in emerging markets. I don't see corruption theoretically; I see it as nineteenth-century illnesses stemming from unsafe water. The contractor who built the water pipes was unqualified (bribed to win the bid), and the subsequent pipe-laying overlapped with sewage systems. I don't see the money laundering pithily portrayed in high-budget TV series. I see North Korea funding brutal oppression, using banks in barely regulated nations to wash gambling and criminally acquired cash. I don't see human rights issues; I see logistics drivers in Myanmar forced to act as minesweepers at gunpoint. I don't see environmental violations; I see death after shoddily constructed hydropower projects collapse.

I am labouring the point intentionally. I don't relate to violations on paper; I see them experientially – and I haven't even got into human and wildlife trafficking. Compliance violations are not financial, white-collar, economic crime, or any other distancing language. They are crimes, infecting entire nations and robbing billions of people of fundamental rights. Corruption is the common denominator in almost all these issues – it is the *how* enabling almost all violations and deserves particular attention.

Maybe, therefore, we need to rethink integrity risk and compliance. That starts with honesty.

Why Now?

Organisational ethics is getting better, isn't it? Looking at whatever feeds you rely on for information will reveal the latest corporate, organisational, or governmental misdeed headlines. We could debate whether that is a function of unethical activity levels or increased societal and journalistic vigilance, but that misses the point. It happens a lot, and we claim we want that to change.

I recently typed "business ethics" into Google and got 380,000,000 results. "Business corruption", a much clunkier phrase, generated 294,000,000 results. Acknowledging that Google – and its results – are not an academic analysis of all public discourse on the topics, that's a rough 56/44% split. If I said to you that 44% of businesses were corrupt, would you agree? Possibly not. So how many are? 30%, 20%, or 5%?

In more relatable terms, 5% of global Gross Domestic Product (GDP) represents an economy the size of Japan or Germany. Big.

I am not guesstimating that a certain percentage of organisations are all bad; I am saying the issue is significant. Any group is an aggregation of people with our collective flaws and limitations. We evolve (hopefully) and learn from our mistakes, creating more tolerant, transparent, and equitable societies. The entities and agencies who employ, serve, and supply us are also learning, but it's not easy. Where do you start?

I don't mind where you start; the journey and destination matter more. We are at an inflection point in many post-industrial economies, where environmental, social, and integrity concerns impact consumer, stakeholder, and employee actions and decisions. In the past few decades, I've seen a trickle (of genuine concern about ethics) turn into a steady stream. The natural inclination for many is to write more policies and create more controls. I prefer to treat people like adults and empower them to make better decisions.

Who Is This Book For?

This book is for those trying to do the right thing, usually with insufficient data, limited resources, and often with recalcitrant or hostile stakeholders. Just because you say no to corruption doesn't mean the local politician won't stick their hand out. It's where honest intention meets risk reality that I focus. I've spent most of my career operating in places where the demand side of risk remains pervasive and robust. It's hard to do the right thing when the decks are stacked; the political framework is inept or corrupt, the judiciary biased and bribed; and competitors don't share your values. That's the bad news. The good news is you're not alone.

I remember the turning point in my career vividly. I was working with a construction and mining firm that had uncovered the potential bribing of public officials in one of their subsidiaries. I was part of a team tasked with interviewing, assessing the risk, and training other subsidiaries. We were running a workshop in Manila. On entering the conference room, I saw a depressingly familiar sight, many large, burly white men with thick gold bracelets and necklaces, arms folded, leaning back, looking hostile. We weren't five minutes into discussing corruption risks when we got the first, "It's *how things are done in The Philippines.*" More came once the one person had opened the floodgates of sweeping national assumptions. Terms like *"these people"* and *"they"* – always an indicator of otherness – reverberated around the hot and drab conference room.

Luckily, after about 30 mins of bashing our heads against hairy-chested "I reckon . . .", *they* spoke. The local finance manager, a Filipina, stood up, banged the table (gently, but enough to get attention), and said, "No, you don't get it. I have to bribe to get down my road to work. I have to pay the doctor for them to see my sick child and the teacher even to grade their papers. I've had enough. If you want to come here, benefit from our resources, the least you can do is bring better standards."

I have wondered about the ethnocentric implications of imposing Western standards of corporate governance on other cultures. In Southeast Asia, where I lived for 12 years, there is a complex history and relationship between former colonisers, now investors and partners. The message is consistent; don't screw us up (again). I have worked with clients from numerous cultures – Japan to Brazil to Israel – and there is broad agreement on the vast majority of what *should* be done. The *how* may differ, but more ethical business practices are not one nation's or one culture's cause.

There is a danger that I talk too much about emerging market risk. In ten years covering the EMEA region, I saw more fraud, human trafficking, and money laundering in London and the United Arab Emirates than in any other country. There is a sort of hierarchy of douchebaggery. Corrupt elites in poorer nations supply resources (including people) that more prosperous nations exploit. The ill-gotten gains and shady deals are concealed offshore and washed in glitzy financial centres. Therefore, the job of ethical culture building is arguably more critical in the established markets, with our distance from the downstream impacts of our (in)actions.

My audience, you, I hope, are organisations and people who want to do the right thing, wherever you are, whatever the circumstances and starting base. You might be working in a large organisation, fighting the good fight, where changing behaviours might feel like trying to turn a battleship in a bathtub. Or maybe you're in a start-up or purpose-driven social business, deciding how to build up your ethical culture and systems to navigate the uncertain seas. It doesn't matter your organisational type or size. I've worked with all sorts; the issues are – to quote Southeast Asia's favourite saying – "Same, but different." The consistent factor: you care about doing the right thing because it is the right thing.

My job is to try and make the risk landscape (and regulation) navigable. So let's begin!

Endnotes

1. Donald R. Cressey, *Other People's Money* (Montclair, NJ: Patterson Smith, 1973), p. 30.
2. https://www.acfe.com/fraud-resources

1
WHO DO YOU WANT TO BE?

If you run an image search for "organisational values wordcloud", you will see similar words. I do this periodically to see what's changed; very little usually. Integrity, ethics, and innovation – or variations thereof – will typically be in most clouds, as will respect, excellence, and inclusion. The similarity in phrasing hollows out the words, leaving them more performative than purpose. I call bullshit, or "Purpass" ("Purparse" for us Brits), the term I coined to denote fake corporate purpose.

Another internet search for average employee satisfaction will produce results that generally herald an engagement rate above 50% as meriting praise. Break out the bunting; only half our employees care. I appreciate I'm taking a leap of logic and faith here, but if significant portions of our workforce are not engaged, they're probably not on board with the mission and values mantra. Fixing this disjoint between what your organisation says and what people feel it does is the first step to effective risk and compliance management.

If you'd told me that five years ago, I'd probably have said, "Hmm, interesting", which is my native British for, "Rubbish, not interesting." I used to be quite sceptical about values, missions, and visions. Too many brand refreshes, replete with swooshes, fonts, and colours, chosen by people in functions that never saw operational realities, made me feel it was all rather cosmetic. Then I got out into the world of small and medium enterprises (SMEs). Talking to people and getting their input is easier when you're smaller. A friend who started a now-booming compliance business providing reporting lines described how his organisation had created their values: they'd asked people! Revelatory.

It's pretty easy to find a list of values, and asking people to vote for their favourites (top 5, for example), takes no time. But are the values all a bit the same? Yes, they are. To illustrate my cynicism, here is a Corporate Values Bingo game (Figure 1.1).

Many of these words have become meaningless and patronising. Are you saying to people, "You're not welcome unless you

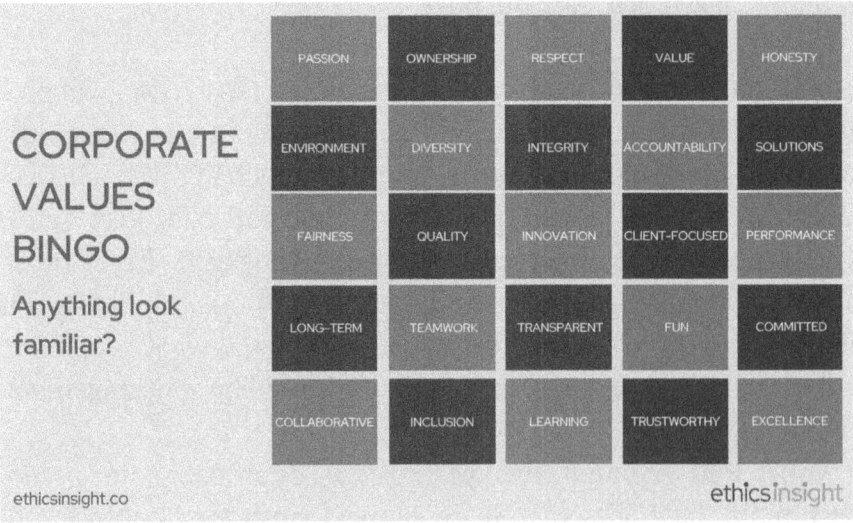

Figure 1.1 Corporate Values Bingo.

are. . ." or saying we ascribe to grand pronouncements without any roadmap to explain *how*? Is it any wonder so many employees are disengaged?

You must demonstrate how you want things done; this should not be a FIFO approach (fit in or F-off). It is more akin to house rules. Are you a shoes on inside, or shoes left at the door kind of organisation? I've lived in Asia most of my working life, and if I had issues with shoes off at the door, I'd not have had much of a social life. It is okay to explain how you want things to be done broadly.

Depending on your organisational size, you may then be able to come together physically or virtually to start that discussion. If you're concerned that stronger personalities – or those in positions of authority – might dominate or stifle the voices of others, good, you should be. Technology can be a democratiser here, even in person. For example, suppose you're trying to compile a list of words that might describe *how* you behave as an organisation. In that case, you can ask people to group them into overlapping or similar concepts. Voting integrity, ethics, respect, transparency, honesty, and honour into a distinct *bucket* will make the next step easier.

At this stage, however, the words are still meaningless. What do these words mean in action? You can ask people to create "doing" sentences. The bucket above might become, "We do the right thing, even when no one is watching." Is that integrity or ethics? Yes. Is it honest? Yes. Is it respect or transparency? Maybe, maybe not. These finer points will stimulate discussion, forcing you all to define actions rather than demonstrate respectful or transparent behaviour. Or perhaps you'll decide transparency isn't your schtick, as might be sensible in some professions where discretion is the currency of credibility.

If you hit an impasse, vote or shelve that topic and move on to the next bucket. After a while, the values start to sort themselves, or more precisely, the lived definition and actions associated with them. Every organisation is seeking to achieve something. Align the values to that. If you're in retail, I'd imagine a customer focus might be primary, whereas, for logistics, it'll be speed and security.

If you're now thinking, "we already have values", good, check back in with your people to see if they all (still) resonate. Your *how* and *what* are not immutable and unchangeable. As societal and political progress, albeit often glacial, moves and changes opinions and challenges perspectives, so should your organisational purpose. You will also need to make sure your ideas translate across cultures. The head of compliance for a large manufacturing company recently told me he had sent a survey about diversity, equity. and inclusion to colleagues in China. They had replied, "This is Western ideals, not relevant here." The Singaporean team at a large UK-listed financial institution also told me that my referencing #MeToo in a training session about ethics was "A Western topic that we don't recognise."

In both instances, and after some digging, the issues were more to do with the medium than the message.

Ideas need to be localised. Every culture I have experienced has its own stories, belief systems, and values. These ethical frameworks overlap more than they ever contradict. If a fan of the Greek and

Roman Stoics read Confucianist or Daoist texts, they'd likely find more that complements than contradicts. What went wrong in the situations above? Do Chinese people not care about inclusion? Are women free of harassment in Singapore? No.

My friend and I had not adapted the message for the local audience. Adapting is as much about finding the right words as allowing people agency. When I asked the Singaporean team what would work better than #MeToo, they replied, "Fairness." Fair enough!

I can already feel some of you squirming. You may be thinking of a decentralised mess where we mangle every message into something locally acceptable, thereby losing meaning or, worse, conflicting with the intention. Moral relativists will point out that we do not understand ethics similarly. You are right, but what's the alternative, misfiring missives with oblique aspirational words greeted with cynicism and rolled eyes?

Having tried to arrive at communal values in the most hostile environments – parents to two terrors – I can assure you it is possible. I've even included how we did it here (Figure 1.2).

We started with a long list of values (the internet is full of such lists). Each member of the family got to choose the five that resonated most. We whittled those choices down to seven words we wanted to turn into sentences. Yes, this involved compromise, but if you allow people to pick five, most of us will cede a couple without too much drama. Then came the significant bit, turning somewhat abstract words that sounded pretentious into lived action, as illustrated by one of the values in Figure 1.3.

	FAMILY	ADVENTURE	FITNESS
	FREEDOM	KINDNESS	KNOWLEDGE
	SECURITY	TEAMWORK	CHANGE
	LOYALTY	COMMUNICATION	PROSPERITY
	CONNECTION	LEARNING	WELLNESS
	CREATIVITY	EXCELLENCE	GRATITUDE
	RESPECT	CONTRIBUTING	GRACE
MAMA	GENEROSITY	SPIRITUALISM	FUN
DADA	INTEGRITY	STRENGTH	JUSTICE
	LOVE	ENTERTAIN	APPRECIATION
ALY	OPENNESS	AFFECTION	WILLINGNESS
LUKE	RESPECT	COOPERATION	PATIENCE
	JOY/PLAY	HUMOUR	FORGIVENESS
	FORGIVENESS	BE TRUE	SELF-RESPECT
	EXCITEMENT	CONTENTMENT	HONOUR
	FAITH	COURAGE	HAPPINESS
	WISDOM	BALANCE	HARMONY
	CARING	COMPASSION	PEACE
	HONESTY		

Figure 1.2 Possible family values.

We wanted to use the active (not passive) voice to give positive meaning and personal ownership. This process stimulated debate and discussion about how we wished to conduct ourselves collectively and individually (and hold each other accountable). Crucially, this was a democratic process. The parents did not get a more significant vote, and the kids hold us accountable (repeatedly!) when our behaviours fall short.

Why did we feel the need to embark on this exercise? Because rule-setting was unwieldy. As parents, we'd seldom remember what rules we'd set, let alone the associated punishment and reward tariffs. The kids probably forgot – or acted as they had – and chaos ensued. We could have codified every expected behaviour, but as an employee of an organisation with a weighty Employee Handbook (or equivalent door-stop) will testify, no one reads rules. Adequately articulated, agreed, and tangible

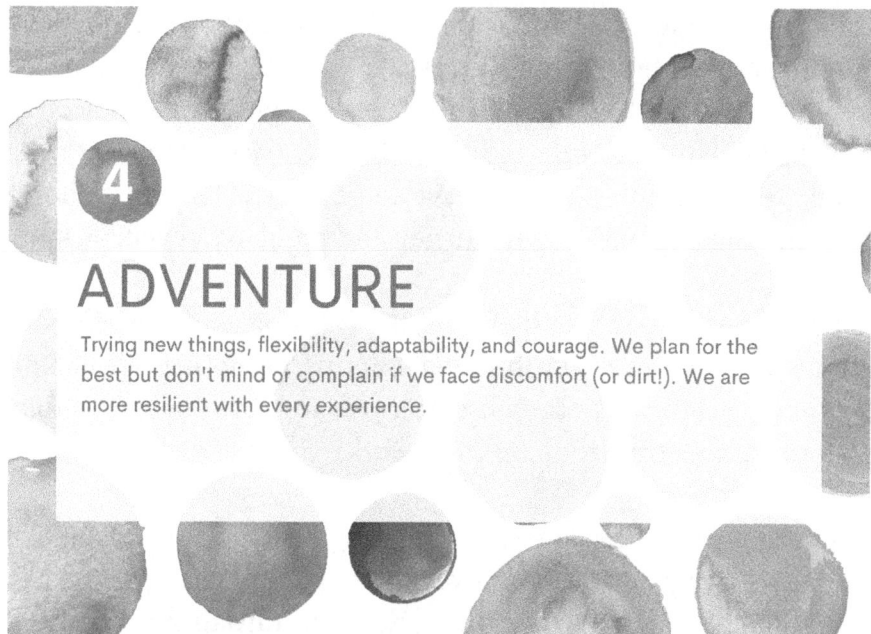

Figure 1.3 Example family value.

statements serve as the first line of defence against unethical behaviours.

Rules, policies, and procedures have their place, but they are the safety net when values have faltered. A moral code at a familial, organisational, or team level provides a framework around which you can hang your rules. For example, if your value is "We deal fairly and honestly with all stakeholders," that is the hook for specificity around fair competition, honest financial reporting, transparent data policies, etc. Without the framework, you have a shopping list of rules that few will read; adherence becomes about an individual's judgement in the absence of guidance, which frequently ends poorly.

If my friend and I had first consulted our colleagues and clients about the intention behind diversity, equity, and inclusion, we might have found an agreed framework. Few people object to broadly held human language around ethics; we tend to want to be good. We want to feel like we have some choice. Give that choice early in your organisational journey and regularly check back in.

Why not write your statements on the front page of a brief document you send out a month or two after people join, with a blank text underneath, and ask your employees to write down how they plan to demonstrate them in their work?

There are several reasons why this might help. Most of us like feeling some agency over our lives and work. For example, a study of just under 1,400 healthcare workers in Taiwan revealed that increased autonomy led to greater job satisfaction and a lower likelihood of leaving their positions.[1] Another study involving 20,000 people, in 2017, by the University of Birmingham, added that autonomy enhanced general well-being and job satisfaction.[2] Asking people to take ownership of their ethics may be more palatable than telling them how to behave.

Furthermore, if we have to author content, we might read it!

Start with Purpose

If deciding what organisation you are (or want to be) is challenging, fear not. That's a good thing. It's like job interviews, where hiring teams ask us to list our best traits or characteristics. There's often dishonesty to that process. The organisation pretends they want "out-of-the-box thinkers" for a role that is mainly spreadsheet jockeying. The candidate plays along, feigning a passionate commitment to and admiration for an organisation they have yet to experience or understand. It's like a mating ritual – not with birds of paradise doing exotic and captivating dances, more like spiders deciding who will eat who. Dispensing with this performance requires courage and honest examination. The employer should, I feel, be straightforward about what the role *actually* entails. The employee should be honest about their expectations and competencies.

This recruiting ritual bears an uncanny resemblance to the disjoint between values and reality at the organisational level. Lofty pronouncements about putting customers at the centre of all we do can quickly become the stuff of ridicule when your frontline customer service representatives hate their boss. Similarly, pledges of integrity and valuing diversity are easily unpicked when tokenism and dodgy dealings are exposed. Employers must expect that employees (and other stakeholders) will not respect the contractual boundaries set unilaterally and (perceived) unfairly. Your average employment contract forbids you from any freedom of genuine expression and opinion about your employer. Poorly done and clumsily, such edicts will not be respected by inhabitants of an ever-more connected and discursive (if also divisive) world. Values set with the hopes of outwardly projecting a culture that does not exist internally are corporate catfishing. Not the bottom-dwelling fish beloved of niche reality TV shows, the process whereby a person creates a fictional persona or fake identity on a social networking or dating service.

If your organisation is a low-cost airline that charges people to relieve themselves, maybe dial back *we care* rhetoric. Instead, it might make more sense to focus on cost, efficiencies, and reliability if they are the currencies of your competition and part of the corporate DNA. At least people (inside and out) will know what to expect. Similarly, if you're an investment bank routinely fined for financing terrorists, criminals, environmental degradation, and other ills, terms like *sustainability* will seem trite. Not everyone will like you if you're authentic, but there's a much greater chance they'll respect you.

Existential questions about your organisational existence extend beyond the realm of risk. For those in risk, legal, or compliance roles, your ability to influence stated values may seem limited. It is still worth raising the point – and the need for a constant examination of purpose – with the powers that be. It's often easier to let employees tell you what they think. Many organisations will use employee engagement (or similar) surveys to help here. Be careful. Some of the common pitfalls include:

1. Asking for too many personal details, rendering assurances of anonymity hollow.

2. Not asking the tough questions.

3. Not sharing the (complete) results.

4. Not doing anything with the results.

I remember one such survey, where the salary band, location, and department disclosure requirements meant I would have been instantly identifiable. I tried to be honest, but I held back a little. The questions are often directed at the organisation, not the person completing the survey. For example, "Do managers uphold standards of excellence?" may seem a good question if excellence is one of your values and critical to what you do. However, it's asking the respondent to make personal judgements about managers they see (including their own). Instead, you may consider asking questions about their experience. You are trying to establish what they feel and think, after all. For example, you might ask for agreement or disagreement to the following statements:

1. I can discuss challenges with my manager.
2. I can speak openly with my manager.
3. My manager helps me.
4. I can ask my team for support.
5. I understand what my manager expects of me.

This non-exhaustive list of statements examines how a manager can create an environment where excellence might be possible. Many other important questions – not least around how valued someone feels – will impact their ability to strive for and attain excellence. The literature on psychological safety is constructive here – and when creating potential surveys. In the context of teams, Amy Edmonson defined psychological safety as "a shared belief held by members of a team that the team is safe for interpersonal risk taking".[3] Psychological safety is an expansive area, but it should be prerequisite reading for anyone managing risk.

To illustrate, we need only consider some reasons for ethical failures. In surveys – including those conducted by the ACFE and the Nordic Business Ethics Network[4] – I read the answers to two questions: (1) why did you not speak up (when you saw wrongdoing)?, and (2) why did you break your ethical principles? I have also asked these questions in risk assessment and training work. Themes emerge, which I might summarise as "I didn't speak up because":

1. I didn't think it would make a difference.

2. I was scared.

3. I didn't think it was my problem (I didn't want to make it my problem).

The responses to questions about compromising our ethics reveal causes including:

1. I was told to (by my manager or someone senior).

2. I feared not hitting targets (time or financial metrics, typically).

3. Everyone else does it.

A theme in all these responses is a lack of psychological safety. We will discuss in detail the speak-up culture later. Still, these statements suggest that when people don't feel they can (safely) raise concerns, have an impact, or admit mistakes, they will be unlikely to uphold whatever values or missions you ascribe. To build a strong risk culture, you need people to take risks! The first such risk is telling you what they feel about your values. Without alignment of values and behaviour, your risk infrastructure has no foundation.

Be purposeful, ambitious, and honest with your values and goals. Those goals should extend to your strategic and financial targets.

Building a culture of integrity is impossible if you're simultaneously setting objectives that require corner-cutting and unethical dealings. If you take nothing else away from this book, set realistic targets if you want to reduce your risk exposure RADICALLY. Most bad ethical decisions stem from fear (of leaders or not hitting targets).

Be Authentic

Why is it such a big deal to have values conflict with reality? Doesn't everyone? Aren't they a statement of what we aspire to? You can manage risk without such alignment, in much the same way an oppressive state rules its citizens – through surveillance and fear. I wouldn't recommend that unless you have deep pockets and a stomach for attrition. Let me give you two examples to illustrate the point.

Unrealistic Targets

A US-headquartered healthcare firm had built a culture of compliance. They had compliance officers and champions, many rules, a glossy code, and practical financial monitoring frameworks.

The regional head of legal & compliance asked me to speak to their Vietnamese subsidiaries' management team. HQ had first tightened rules around gifts given to healthcare professionals (HCPs, doctors mostly), and the local team responded by taking them out to nice dinners and lunches. When that was banned, they moved to pay HCPs to speak at conferences. The iron fist of compliance squelched that ruse.

Next, an expensive claim came across my client's desk for thousands of dollars to "rent a room for an hour". Upon enquiry, the legal & compliance head realised that HCPs, so indignant at "compliance" clamping down on gifts and entertainment, demanded a steep "rental fee" to use a theatre in the hospital to demo the products.

You've probably realised that influencing HCPs through such payments and entertainment is slightly off. The local management team retorted, "Well, you didn't have a policy banning it [exorbitant 'rental' agreements]."

The issue was clear; no one thought of values or ethics, "How might this be perceived? What is our intention here? Is this the right thing to do?" Policing organisations that require you to prohibit every possible misdeed in some policy or missive is exhausting and ineffective. We will cover some situations where specificity and well-documented rules are necessary; for example, the right thing is not immediately obvious (like complex anti-competition or data privacy regulations). However, understanding or estimating intention (or motive) is essential in most risk areas. What did we, or the source of threat (adversary), hope to achieve? In this example, when pressed, the local management team struggled to explain how renting a room for a couple of hours could or should cost thousands of dollars. What was the intention of the HCPs? Presumably to get money where once were gifts, lavish dinners, and handsome speaking engagement fees. What was the goal of the sales representatives? To get the HCPs to buy, even if that meant paying them off. Did anyone need rules to see this was wrong?

Realistic Targets

A few years prior, just as Myanmar opened to the world (2011 or thereabouts), I met a Japanese heavy equipment manufacturer's APAC management team. We were running a workshop on ethics and compliance.

They had very little by way of a policy or monitoring framework. We asked them how they assessed and managed risk as they'd had remarkable success at avoiding the challenges that befall many others in their sector. Their leading salesperson described a prospect in Myanmar who had recently asked them to provide excavators and bulldozers. The salesperson had flown to Myanmar and "kicked the tyres." He told his regional CEO, "We shouldn't bid; these guys are cowboys." They didn't respond to the tender. A few weeks later, the prospective client bulldozed monks protesting environmental degradation at the mine site. The media carried photos of my client's competitor's vehicle, the weapon in the multiple murders. I asked the CEO how he'd agreed to the salesperson's recommendation and passed up on what would have been a lucrative contract. His reply was telling, "I trust my people to do the right thing."

You can manage risk well with limited infrastructure if you have clear and consistent values, hire the right people, empower them, and back them up.

The Japanese firm did, of course, have procedures to document business decisions. They also informally discussed risk when discussing what projects to (not) pursue. The difference with the

HCP example was that values and ethics led to decisions, not the ticking of boxes in compliance with rules.

Most organisations sit between these two examples. The trick is striking the balance of autonomy and control that works for you. This balance may be further complicated by workforce composition and demographic differences in larger organisations. Attitudes to instruction, hierarchy and critical feedback may vary widely across globalised firms. The analogy that makes sense is the equaliser on digital stereos (I know, I'm giving away my age). You can alter the frequency and timbre, but you must play the same song.

How do you choose the right song? You could try the experiment we did as a family. Doing so may not be as difficult as it first seems. Logic-based and advanced surveying tools, or even interactive feedback tools like Mentimeter,[5] help assess our thoughts and feelings at scale quickly. As ever, the devil is in the detail. We must allow space for nuance. Asking people if integrity is essential as a binary (yes/no) question will generally elicit an overwhelming response in the affirmative. However, it may not be their first choice if you ask them to rank a list of values – one of which is integrity.

Furthermore, you might see more qualified responses if you ask, "How important is integrity?" on a Likert scale (from unimportant to essential). As I said, authenticity is vital. For example, have you ever been to a mechanic or called out a repairperson for a broken home appliance and heard the ominous *sharp-intake-of-breath-through-pursed-lips*? This phenomenon is usually followed by obfuscating or deliberately complex language – interspersed with jargon or the names of obscure widgets – and then a hefty quote. What about the adverts that say, "Hurry, limited stock"? Or the real estate agent who claims another buyer is putting together an offer for that dream home just outside your intended budget. Of course, there are artisans, mechanics, salespeople, and realtors with impeccable integrity and honesty. Not every positive word – like integrity, honesty, transparency, kindness – may authentically resonate with your organisation, so don't fake it.

We respond to genuine much better than we react to performative. Choose authenticity, but recognise this is just the start of the journey towards ethically and appropriately managing risk.

Where Does Risk Fit In?

Let's also consider risk when deciding what kind of organisation you want to be. It is everywhere, and most good opportunities live on the other side of fear and risk. We must, therefore, define our risk appetite.

Risk appetite and risk tolerance can confuse people at first. The former is typically more qualitative, and the latter is given the veneer of quantitative (even if that is an estimation). Let me explain with a scenario. Your company, Startup Sensation, might decide certain risks are not worth taking as they could cause significant damage to the business. The operative word is significant, which varies depending on what you do and with whom.

Let's say Startup Sensation sells ethically sourced vegan products. Significant damage might stem from links to animal (or human) rights violations. Startup Sensation's leadership team may deploy risk management resources to supply chain transparency and ethical sourcing. Startup Sensation could elect to expend fewer resources on fraud risk management; perhaps they feel purpose-driven people are less likely to defraud them. The leadership might qualify the risk tolerance as near-zero per cent for animal rights violations in the supply chain and decide they won't accept fraud risks above 3% of revenue.

If you think this doesn't make much sense, I'd agree. Risk appetite and tolerance are very useful when you're a mega-corporation with data and resources to model and estimate most things. It's handy if your business lends itself to qualitative analysis, for example, a financial services business where fines, fraud, and human error can be qualified and quantified (within reason).

Now, if Startup Sensation sold discounted (factory outlet priced) goods online, relying on warehouses in low-cost locations with lower-cost workers, the tolerances might be flipped. In this scenario, they may care less about ethical purchasing and more about fraud impacting tight margins. Maybe the leadership team would spend no time vetting suppliers and much more time monitoring employees, packaging areas, returns, refunds, suspicious purchasing patterns, and more.

To deal with the confusion, you can go one of two ways: (1) get all ISO; or (2) keep it simple. The ISO path (in particular ISO 31000 – Risk Management[6]) defines risk appetite as "the amount and type of risk that an organization is prepared to pursue, retain or take". Risk tolerance sets the parameters and variation (often in percentage terms) within each risk (e.g., returns of faulty goods of less than 1% of revenue). If your eyes are glazing over, maybe this model is more straightforward:

1. **Risk appetite**: What kind of organisation are we?

2. **Risk tolerance**: How will we know if we're on track?

If you've established your organisational purpose and values, it should be more straightforward than considering the entire risk universe in abstraction. For the vegan products, trust (in the origin of the products), treatment of your employees, and customer service should probably be areas of low-risk appetite. The risk tolerance will become the flipside of your promises; for example, if you advertise your products as "100% cruelty-free", you'd better damn well have the risk controls to ensure 0% of that in your supply chain. Similarly, you could measure employee treatment with psychological safety assessments, engagement surveys, turnover rates, employment disputes (unfair dismissal, harassment, discrimination, etc.), and exit interview data, to name a few.

I am covering a lot of ground very quickly here, intentionally. My experience of risk appetite and tolerance is that they're pointless unless you understand the frontline risks your organisation experiences, the focus of much of this book. You may wish to return to these areas once your risk universe is clearer.

Be Purposeful

Just because many organisations fail to live up to their values and mission statements have become a joke (in many cases) doesn't mean they're worthless. In my mind, they are not some brainwashed mantra to be uttered by subjugated drones; they are your purpose. If that is to make as much money as possible, screw those pesky customers and employees, then keep values focused on profit, efficiencies, and cost reduction. Be authentic, get opinions from within, and make sure you have the right building blocks for the cultural, governance, and strategic infrastructure you will build around them.

Endnotes

1. Blossom Yen-Ju Lin, Yung-Kai Lin, Cheng-Chieh Lin, and Tien-Tse Lin, Job Autonomy, Its Predispositions and Its Relation to Work Outcomes in Community Health Centers in Taiwan, *Health Promotion International*, 28(2) (2013), 166–177. https://doi.org/10.1093/heapro/dar091.
2. D. Wheatley, Autonomy in Paid Work and Employee Subjective Well-Being, *Work and Occupations*, 44(3) (2017), 296–328. https://doi.org/10.1177/0730888417697232.
3. Amy Edmondson, Psychological Safety and Learning Behavior in Work Teams. *Administrative Science Quarterly*, 44(2) (1999), 350–383. https://doi.org/10.2307/2666999.
4. https://www.nordicbusinessethics.com/survey/
5. https://www.mentimeter.com/
6. https://www.iso.org/iso-31000-risk-management.html

2
LIVING UP TO YOUR PROMISES

The real work begins, turning your purpose into practical (and concise) guidance. We learn and relate to information differently. There is no perfect solution to communicating your expectations across the organisation. There are a few hacks, however.

Don't be too shy (or proud) to beg, steal, and borrow from other parts of your organisation. For example, if health, safety, and environment (HSE) is a more mature part of the risk function, look at how they communicated messages, socialised expectations, and set frameworks. HSE content and culture are borrowable because (typically) they are straightforward. That level of "wear a hard hat at all times while on-site" may seem simplistic for ethics and compliance issues (which can get complex), but my rule is if I can't explain it to a 10-year-old child, so they understand it, I'm not explaining it clearly enough. HSE does clear guidance pretty well, usually.

Other teams with lessons to teach might include information security, quality assurance, and marketing. Good information security guidance doesn't waste time explaining how a computer works or the intricacies of firewall breaches; they focus on behaviours. The message might be "don't stick thumb drives into your laptop" or "only click links to legitimate and known sites". In ethics and compliance especially, many feel the need to explain their workings; few of us care. Have you ever sat through a compliance training session where the various violations under a given law were poured over in gruesome and unflinchingly dull detail? Most of us have. Understanding the adequate procedures defence to the UK's Bribery Act 2010 may be helpful knowledge for the board (and select other senior leaders). If your objective is to tell salespeople to stop wining and dining clients to win business, talk through those scenarios instead. Focus on the behaviours that drive the issues, not the legal ramifications. Making training stick we will cover later, but remember, the medium is the message.

Quality assurance for many organisations is essential. Contamination, failure, liability, injury, and death are words no one wants to hear. How do you ensure those words don't materialise with respect to your organisation? I imagine it's not through lengthy policies written in legalese or interminable training videos featuring out-of-work actors walking at diagonals across the screen as they talk confidently to the camera. Typically, one might assure quality through a blend of simple frameworks, concise, and user-relevant training, with supervision and testing. Look at these systems and processes and see what you can borrow.

Finally, marketing (or the equivalent function) will have much to teach about relatability. These folks will speak the language of impressions, reactions, click-through, and engagement rates. Marketing will know how long people linger on certain intranet pages, what types of emails get read, whether people click links or prefer embedded content, etc. Beyond your organisation, what resonates with customers? There is no shame in using attention-grabbing, pithy, or witty content to get across your (serious) points; generally, it's preferable.

A friend of mine, currently the Chief Compliance Officer for a large logistics firm, described the best compliance officer he'd ever met. The organisation was in disarray (from a compliance perspective), and they took the unusual decision to appoint someone with a marketing background as the new officer. He embarked on a world tour of the various global subsidiary companies with a simple presentation about compliance; one slide, with his mobile phone number. The message was clear; before the organisation could resolve issues, they needed to understand why they kept occurring. The simplest way was to build trust; a senior executive giving you their direct line seemed a quick way to generate that. My friend, Charles, explained how this taught him a second vital lesson: brevity. Charles explained that with every new regulation, he made it his mission to ensure that little of the legal language from the guidance made it into any of his policies or communications. Why is this excellent advice? Google anti-competition law, wherever you are, and then try and read the legislation to the nearest 10-year-old. Let me know how you get on.

Or, you could explain to that same precocious (I've yet to meet a 10-year-old that isn't!) primary-schooler the concepts using classroom dynamics. It might work better. For example, would it be fair if a small group of students blocked access to the swings during break-time? In legal speak, this might be the denial of market access. If those same students copied each other's answers during tests, your 10-year-old advisor might say that was unfair (or collusion, in grown-up speak). I'm not suggesting you distil complex law into child-centric examples, more that you communicate the core of the message succinctly and in a format people can follow. In other words, a call to action – a central component of most marketing campaigns.

In later chapters, we'll cover communication and training strategies (that work), but first, you need to set realistic expectations around living up to your promises.

Zero Tolerance = Zero Clue

I am sure you have heard the phrase "zero tolerance". It is used in numerous settings, from law enforcement to school bullying to compliance. In all cases, it's at best unwise and at worst highly damaging. I am not suggesting we tolerate unpleasant and potential criminal behaviour. I'm arguing that zero tolerance loses trust and prevents people from coming forward.

I have worked on many investigations but have responded to more allegations and reports (often channelled through a whistle-blower or speak-up line). When you interview someone brave enough to make a report, you often realise many others chose to stay silent; why? It's hard to know precisely, but my anecdotal experience suggests the most common reasons are:

1. I was scared.

2. I didn't think it would make a difference.

3. It didn't seem that important.

Fear as a deterrent to speaking up we will unpack in due course. The other reasons often link to zero tolerance if you talk to witnesses (who chose not to come forward). You have set an incredibly high bar if you claim that you will respond with full force to every violation and not tolerate infractions. Imagine if law enforcers said they had a 100% conviction record; would that fill you with confidence? Or would you think this sounds like North Korea? It is impossible to secure confessions (or sufficient evidence) on every case and allegation. Let me give you a few examples of issues I've seen.

A manufacturing company fired a senior employee for harassment. So enraged at his treatment, he threatened to go to the competition authorities with evidence he claimed to possess of "significant violations" involving his erstwhile employer. He made this allegation, having been ejected from the office and his laptop confiscated. The overzealous IT team wiped the computer immediately, readying it for the next person through the door. What should you now do if you have a policy claiming zero tolerance for anti-competitive practices? Fire him twice? With what evidence? He claims to have plenty, but you wiped his computer. To complicate matters, in that country (South Korea), the authorities offer witnesses and whistleblowers on anti-competition issues immunity from prosecution. Your chances of securing access and interviews with the subject (outside of a courtroom) are limited.

What about a female contractor (a security guard) alleging that an employee exposed himself to her repeatedly? What if the female contractor did not consent to an interview? Supplementary research suggested that the employee implicated had been the subject of other inappropriate allegations, but the lack of witnesses hampered the investigation. What does zero tolerance tell you to do here? Fire the employee without evidence or due process?

These examples are necessarily simplified, and we looked at the logical investigative avenues (IT forensics, CCTV review, interviewing proximate witnesses). However, you will lose people's trust if you set your prosecutorial bar at a zero failure rate.

Harsh-sounding non-compliance rhetoric may force people to downplay the seriousness of an issue. Let's choose another example; let's say a new joiner, who is black, is not invited to team building nights out. The new employee challenges his supervisor, who replies, "We go to country and western bars; we didn't think it would be your thing." You would probably want more data to arrive at a prognosis and establish the subtext and intent of the supervisor's statement.

Now put yourself in the new employee's position; would you speak up? Let me qualify that. Would you come forward if the company has a zero-tolerance policy for racism? What if the supervisor is otherwise supportive and friendly, albeit emotional and culturally challenged? If you fear the supervisor might be fired, you may decide "it's not that important". But it is. These things make workplaces toxic. You need to have appropriate (and flexible) frameworks that allow escalation of concerns without the imminent threat of stiff penalties and enforcement.

Finally, zero tolerance can be and has been misused. We all make mistakes. I have seen instances where over-zealous or politicised punishment of non-compliance has destroyed trust in the risk and compliance function.

A few years back, an oil and gas equipment manufacturer invited a client for a factory site visit. The client arrived in Indonesia (from Singapore) and applied for a visa. Indonesian permits, especially related to technical work visits, can be complicated. The immigration official, sensing an opportunity to extract a corrupt payment, claimed she needed a different visa and detained the client in a cell. Understandably panicked, she called the manufacturer's country manager requesting help. He duly spoke to the officials who requested a "fee" to settle the issue and allow his client safe passage. He paid, which was the wrong thing to do from a compliance standpoint, but an understandable human decision as he was dealing with a distressed and angry client.

An internal investigation followed, and the zero tolerance for bribery was used as a pretext to fire the country manager. When I visited the facility – with a brief to understand how other similarly risky interactions might be better managed – the whole office was terrified. Extortive requests from officials are the norm in some parts of Indonesia's bureaucracy. Without the safe space to admit as much, no one wanted to make any decisions, paralysing the business.

In the Indonesian case, the clumsy and ill-conceived application of non-compliance penalties was not malicious. In other instances, it is. I have seen managers use technicalities of non-compliance to force people out of jobs. Often those targeted are speaking out against unethical conduct. For instance, a project engineer observed how bribes to win bids had seen woefully unqualified contractors appointed to an infrastructure project. The region was reeling from an earthquake that had left citizens without safe water. So bad was the work that the water was contaminated, and the engineer estimated the tunnels would soon collapse, possibly causing fatalities and landslides. He raised these concerns. His employers threatened him with dismissal (they were in on the corrupt plot), but he continued. Eventually, his superiors used a minor instance of timesheet non-compliance as grounds for firing him.

The water project case is not an outlier. A simple internet search, especially with keywords including "tech sector" and "employee harassment", reveals that performative or ineffectual zero-tolerance frameworks are common.

In summary, recognise that committing to zero tolerance – or another similarly sweeping and all-encompassing phrase – will not work because:

1. It is unrealistic and sets you up for failure.

2. Violations are not binary; they're on a sliding scale.

3. It allows little space for restorative justice.

4. It can be a deterrent to people coming forward.

5. All too often, it's performative (showing off to regulators and investors).

What's the alternative? Be honest and explain you do your best, which is an evolving process and be open to feedback. Then be as transparent as you can be about the process and findings. That notion can make people fidgety and nervous (lawyers especially), but the best lessons and learnings come from actual events, not fictitious scenarios.

To be clear, I am not advocating leniency for the more severe violations. I suggest realism and honesty with your people around the consequences of failing to live up to your values.

Managing Reasonable Expectations

Now the real work begins: reasonableness. For the legally minded among you, this will be a very familiar concept. The reasonableness test is a staple of various laws and statutes; it is also subjective. For lovers of specificity, this may be frustrating, but it's your friend.

Early in my career, I sat through a surprisingly non-torturous presentation by the Financial Conduct Authority (FCA), a UK financial services regulatory body. It was the early 2000s, and other attendees raised objections about the lack of clarity in specific regulations. The speaker, whose name sadly escapes me, replied, "We didn't want to draw a straight line in the sand; we wanted a wiggly one. If you've ever tried to trace a wiggly line, it's not easy. Our decision was intentional; stay well on the right side of the line."

The concept was a sound one, ignoring the FCA's abject failures related to the flows of corrupt and dirty money into the UK. It's one I've used frequently since. For example, if two countries have laws on the same topic – let's say, bribery – and one prohibits private and public bribery, and the other only public corruption, which do you pick? Do you adhere to different laws in different markets? Or do you decide that bribery is generally not a great foundation to build a business and choose the higher watermark (farther from the wiggly line)?

Your colleagues want to be reasonable. Few of us set out to be the baddie in the documentary movie of our life in which we are the star. Managing reasonable expectations is explaining that lines can sometimes be hard to trace and err on the side of caution. This approach is sometimes called a culture of ethics (distinct from a culture of compliance). We will unpack some ethical decision-making frameworks in due course, but you want to encourage people to ask questions for now.

The first step to walking your values and building a culture of genuine (not performative) integrity is to discuss what that looks like in daily decisions. If you think this sounds cumbersome and like it will slow down decision-making, it's not really. You probably already have meetings to discuss what to do (about almost everything). A "Have we discussed the risks or potential consequences?" question is not a massive task. You're already doing it, maybe not all the time or for the risks we'll discuss in this book.

At this stage, it may help to define reasonable expectations of employees (and other stakeholders). Typically, this might take the form of a Code of Conduct, Code of Business Ethics, or something else with the word Code in it.

Your Code

Ah, the Code. Never in the writing field has so much time been spent, by so many, on something so few read. Ask most people what's in their organisation's Code, and they'll probably say, "Rules 'n' stuff", before shrugging their shoulders and pushing up their lower lip to make a feigned confused frowny face.

They might reference the introduction from a CEO (or equivalent) they have never met, usually a grey dude in a dark suit. You're thinking, why would they not read something I am selling so well?

Because it's usually dull boilerplate rubbish, a recent experiment – to try and find clear decision-making frameworks – in various Codes of large organisations confirmed the issue. Most decision-making frameworks start with "We always obey the law" – oh, yeah, slow clap. The basis of your ethics is avoiding criminality; please stop it. You're dreaming too big. The next step might read, "We always follow the Code and our policies [which no one reads]." Now, where's my prize?

Codes are desperately dull and lack any thought of their audience. Most of your colleagues are not experts on the law. Saying that you expect people to follow the law leaves a lot to be interpreted (often wrongly). Most folks will recognise that stealing is against the law. Still, they'll have a more challenging time determining the legal framework on data privacy, anti-competition, appropriate waste disposal, cybersecurity, or numerous other areas that most organisations must contend with. Secondly, the law is a safety net, not a moral benchmark. We need to aim higher than what we *could* do to consider what we *should* do.

A good Code talks to the reader. What is it we do (as an organisation)? How do we treat one another? Where might we face unethical, legal, or other pressures? What do we ask you to do about that? Who can you speak to if you're aware of a possible issue? Throughout these questions, succinct scenarios from within your organisation can bring the Code to life.

I wanted to spell out what a good Code should look like, but that's tricky when it has to be bespoke to your organisation. The best I can do is this:

1. Introduce the issue in a line or two. For example, a conflict of interest is where your interests might compromise your decisions or judgement in the workplace.

2. Explain the common areas (of confusion): How and what (possible conflicts of interest) to disclose.

3. Explain what you want people to do.

4. Give an example or two.

5. Direct them to any further resources.

6. Have a simple key to explain who needs to know (not all Code issues are relevant to all employees).

7. Tell them where to go if they have a question, comment, or concern.

If you think this will make documents epic, potentially, in this long form, it will. Using the miracle of graphic design and imagery, you can fit anywhere from two to four areas of your Code on a landscape-oriented PDF page.

Taking a step back, you might wonder what sage has the answers to points 2 and 4. Yes, the team(s) responding to possible issues can help, but so will employees working in frontline roles. My best anecdotes always come from frontline stories. I'll tell you the one I heard this afternoon. An insurance assessor visited a policyholder who claimed a $200,000 excavator had gone missing;

"poof" just vanished. This visit was not the assessor's first rodeo; they researched the make and model. Upon arriving, the assessor's first question was, "What colour is it?" An interesting opener. The policyholder replied, "Yellow, I think." A fair guess, given many excavators are yellow or orange. Unfortunately, this model only came in white, a less common colour. The policyholder withdrew the claim shortly afterwards. This story won't add much to a Code, but it demonstrates that case studies and actual situations are better teachers than pages of theory; in this case, preparing for investigative interviews is essential. These accounts can also inject a modicum of humour, which tends to be more memorable.

Crowdsource your content; it will be more relatable and actionable for your readers. Then have a clear "Call To Action" (CTA). I will repeatedly return to this concept, as risk and compliance doctrine is often couched in the pastime of fence-sitting. Give an opinion, and give your colleagues a CTA.

There can be an understandable temptation to get the Code together quickly. Typically, this might include researching a few competitors' or sector-relevant versions and picking and choosing what you like. That makes a lot of sense, but be careful. When I was about 12 years old, my school, to make us less feral and more valuable members of society, decided it would be a great idea if we learned the basics of garment-making. I believed my dad would appreciate silk boxer shorts (he didn't). One fabric was not enough for this endeavour. Best to choose about seven different patterns, a riot of colour, in my mind at least. Other materials also react differently to different stitching techniques. The lopsided and scratchy result lasted one round in the washing machine, emerging as a slew of soon-to-be dusting cloths. Don't make your Code like my dad's boxer shorts.

If you want to draw inspiration from the work of others, and why not, treat it more like an interior designer might. Sketch out how each room in your house – each area of the Code – looks for you. Where are there lights (additional content and training support), the doors (where to go for help), and who lives in each room? Now take those snippets from others' Codes and work out how you'll need to adapt them for your home. I've seen this done well by a select few. They all had a plan – a framework or floorplan – where they needed to place fixtures, fittings, and furnishings.

I have created template Codes in the past, and they have their place. Typically that place is when trying to tick a box – often as part of a tender or a client onboarding process – where you don't have weeks or months to draft your organisation-specific version. Even in these situations, the template Codes are built with adaptation – to reflect those issues that matter to you. Whether your Code is a work of art or a template needing refining, the good news is you've taken your first step, and it's probably better than the vast majority of legalese dirges out there!

Who Follows the Code?

Now you have a Code (or something similar). Who needs to know? This question may seem obvious, and you might be thinking, "Our people, duh!" True, but that is a big assumption. In many organisations, Codes are not universally accepted or recognised.

The senior leadership team might view the Code as the framework for employees (an autocratic but not uncommon view). Those subject to that yoke will likely view the Code as performative rubbish. Laws – and a Code is your internal legal system – are unpopular when they are enforced unevenly (or worse, politically and selectively).

Your first task, which can be challenging, is to explain that even venerable and lofty boards are subject to the Code's provisions. A less aggressive way to do this might be to ask members of the board (or your version) to own sections of the Code and communicate what it means to them. Senior leaders talking through their challenges and dilemmas humanises "them" to the "us" and enhances understanding. Teaching others has been proven to be one of the most effective ways to internalise knowledge – infinitely better than reading![1]

One of the better examples I saw in a giant telecommunications company involved simple self-shot videos by executive committee members talking about an "ethics moment" they had faced and how the Code had helped them. These approaches may also help frontline employees recognise that (most) senior leaders once met the same risks they now manage. Conversely, if you have leaders who have no clue about the frontline – which remains a depressingly familiar situation – keep them away from such initiatives, as they will do more harm than good.

With your internal Code coverage a bit clearer, you may now wish to decide how far the framework should extend. For instance, will you ask contractors, temporary workers, or consultants to comply? What about third-party providers? By third parties,

I mean any organisation with whom you have contractual or commercial relationships. If this sounds daunting or shocking, it isn't. I run a small business, and I am surprised when we are *not* asked to sign documents with Code in the title. Often these frameworks are a variation of the original – condensed and catered for the exposure we pose to our client or partner. It should be logical which elements of the Code are relevant to external parties, but we will explain how to manage external stakeholders later.

If you extend your Code to others, you also make it clear how and where (and to whom) they can ask questions or report concerns.

The Mood in the Middle

If you've encountered ethics and compliance language before, you may have heard the phrase "the tone from the top" or something along those lines. If leaders don't walk the talk, then you can't expect others to. It's a very sound principle, and myriad idioms point to the downside (where this doesn't happen), notably, the Chinese proverb "the fish rots from the head".

We talked about getting those leaders on board in the previous section, but we also need to consider the mood in the middle; how the managers (or similar operational leadership functions) feel about your Code, values, and organisation. You've probably heard the maxim, "people don't leave companies; they leave managers". While such a simplistic analysis of multifaceted choices is misleading, there is some truth in it. Rubbish managers pollute cultures. In various surveys and my anecdotal experience, one of the top three reasons for ethical failures is, "I was following the instructions from my manager." It should be no surprise that the person with the most influence over your day-to-day can also have the most significant negative impact.

Therefore, understanding how your middle management feels about the Code (and your values) is an essential step to functional integrity. We discussed starting your values with purpose, and I offered a few questions that might help you understand how your people feel. Those questions again:

1. I can discuss challenges with my manager.

2. I can speak openly with my manager.

3. My manager helps me.

4. I can ask my team for support.

5. I understand what my manager expects of me.

If you're asking these questions, some possible additions or variations might include:

1. I understand what is expected of me.

2. My team knows what is expected of us.

3. My manager trusts me.

4. I feel safe making decisions.

5. I feel safe making a mistake.

6. I can ask my team for help.

7. In my team, we are all accountable for our actions.

8. Work is allocated fairly.

9. My team accepts different people.

10. My work is valued.

This list is by no means exhaustive, and you will need to adapt it to your organisation. The objective is simple, to understand how your people feel. Feelings get a bad rap in many business circles where rationality must prevail, right? Nope! Think back to the last time you bought insurance, was it a sanguine and analytical process or were emotions driving you? We can kid ourselves with our thinking, but our feelings are harder to manufacture. If you've ever tried to feel a contrary emotion to what you're experiencing, you'll know how challenging it can be. These more personally phrased questions are designed to understand the respondent's lived experience. Asking us to psychologically profile our manager – with the usual "my manager is . . ." statements – forces us to estimate the person's state and intentions. It's much simpler to just ask us how *we* feel.

Be careful about the identifiers you ask if you decide to go down some form of surveying or canvassing route. You must allow people the anonymity that encourages honesty. Once you have your results, you may find a few things. Some teams will be toxic but seemingly performing well – look for burnout here and losing some of your best talent. Other groups will be contented under-achievers – maybe the managers are too much friendly and too little pace-setting. There will be bright spots of happy and high-achieving folks, as there will be the reverse.

As a risk or ethics and compliance professional, your role is to recognise where managers might be abusing their positions and where employees feel disengaged or angry. Abusive managers seldom stop at making lives miserable; they might feel empowered to take other liberties (here you find corruption, anti-competitive behaviours, discrimination, and harassment). Fed-up employees will often feel little loyalty to your cause. In these conditions, fraud (including petty theft) and conflicts of interest (especially side-hustles) sprout like mushrooms in a damp and dingy forest.

If my simplified prognosis sounds bleak, don't worry; knowing where to start your work is a gift. As one friend – then the compliance officer for Asia-Pacific for a healthcare company – put it, "I just want a system that tells me, 'This is what you need to work on today, start here', because there's so much I could do, it's overwhelming." Knowing where to start is a blessing.

Risk Assessments

I wouldn't call analysis of the tone at the top or the mood in the middle a risk assessment, as it's much more than that; it's a cultural roadmap to reach the consumers of your risk and compliance content. The analogy that makes sense to me is a culture MRI – helping us understand if there are any underlying (and not always visible) issues and where we're nice and healthy. The risk assessment is like the health check and lifestyle questions before the MRI.

Turning from this metaphor to your organisation, we start by considering the risk factors seemingly outside your control (country and sector) before considering those we might have some agency over:

1. **Country risks** include the rule of law, the security situation, the government commitment to integrity, public sector corruption, attitudes towards business (and foreign investment), respect for human rights, geopolitical disputes, and freedoms (personal, media, and of association).

2. **Sector risks** overlap with country risks and may include industry-specific exposures (e.g., financial services to money laundering or manufacturing to modern slavery). Other stakeholders (including industry bodies, competitors, and regulators) will further impact your operations in areas including intellectual property protection, data privacy, and environmental protections.

3. **Operational risks** consider the day-to-day issues, including environmental and social impact, ease of doing business, security (cyber and physical), licensing and permitting.

4. **Routes to market risks** consider the extent to which you rely on public procurement, your customers' expectations (gifts, entertainment, offshore structures, donations, etc.), your reliance and use of intermediaries (agents, distributors, and alike), business partners, and funders.

These lists are far from exhaustive, but they get you started. We're mapping what you do, where you do it, how you do it, with whom, when, and why.

Listing all these stakeholders and interactions may seem onerous – and it's not easy – but you can get 80% of the way there in a couple of hours of focused (group) work. If you need help, ask me. These initial hours invested will be invaluable as you build a right-sized program, matching your operational realities. If I go back to the MRI analogy, imagine trying to live a life where you protect yourself from all risks without considering how your environment, lifestyle, and genetics might impact your well-being.

I've used a whiteboard, or the fancier online and interactive tools, to facilitate this exercise by starting with those simple questions. Write a "Who you deal with" column and ask your colleagues to list all those stakeholders and interactions. Next, you can ask "Why?"; this is an excellent question as it should be easy to answer; for instance, we deal with this joint venture as it is mandatory in that country to have a local content partner. If it's harder to answer a *why*, dig deeper, some of these interactions may indicate legacy redundancies, but they can also suggest collusive, corrupt, or otherwise problematic dependencies.

When questions help us understand a few things, including dependence, leverage, and criticality. Do not assume infrequent means less critical – maybe you deal with the agency that licenses your products once a year, but you can't do business without their approval. "When" questions help us determine what interactions sit on our critical path and could derail operations if they go south.

What you do may seem self-explanatory, but it significantly impacts risk. If you hold reams of sensitive government data, you're likely of greater interest to hackers than if you are a garments wholesaler. But the wholesaler likely has more downstream risk exposure to human rights (including modern slavery) abuses in their supply base.

The way you phrase questions here will be essential. My experience – and I understand it's also the subject of many studies – suggests that we struggle with terminology. Many risk assessments are built on a matrix with probability/likelihood on one axis and impact/consequences on the other. Then you will see words like "almost certain" to "rare" and "severe" to "negligible". It will be no surprise that we get perplexed picking the correct ranking. The data you discover will also confuse you, as you'll wonder if people's perception of risk differs on a given issue or if their perception of word meaning differs.

A safer approach, always, is to use simple language. For example, "Demands for bribes are common during tenders", with a 5-point Likert sliding scale from "strongly disagree" to "strongly agree". If you get varied responses here, you know it's about the perception of the risk issue (which is a helpful indicator; are we too cautious or too cavalier about this risk?), not people struggling with terminology. I like numbers. Estimating in percentage terms avoids all linguistic subjectivity and is universally translatable. We also tend to be more accurate at the median numerical point. What about impact?

Impact is the Pandora's box of risk. Let's stay with the tender bribery risk to illustrate the challenge. What impact are we assessing? The impact of paying the bribe? The impact of paying the bribe and an employee raising this internally? The impact of the media uncovering your dodgy deal? What is the impact of a regulator finding out (if so, which one)? The impact of not paying the bribe and losing the bid? You get the point. Those questions lead to more, including investigative costs, fines, jail time, lost business, lost revenue, cancelled contracts, debarments, low employee morale, business disruption, no client retention, etc. Many organisations try to quantify these risks in terms of lost revenue, remediation costs, share price, and other metrics. It's a bit like trying to estimate the impact of a fire in your home – it depends.

A better way to think of impact, for me at least, is to consider harm to people and the planet. For those integrity risks that may not be immediately evident, the next question should be, "Is the process impacted by the risk critical?" For example, if we establish a high(er) probability of bribe requests during tenders, ask if such tenders are essential to your business. If so, that's a high-risk event, and you'll need to plan ways to win work cleanly. Don't overcomplicate it; you will already have a good sense of impact from the when, why, and what questions; listen for words like "frequent", "critical path", "mandatory", "fundamental", "essential", etc. Low, medium, and high work perfectly well if you're trying to think of a scale to measure impact.

Test out your framework on unsuspecting friends and family. We manage risk daily (driving a car, personal security, swiping right, ordering late-night kebabs, asking elderly relatives about immigration), so pick an example and roll with it.

If you're considering external data sources, there are loads of resources ranking country and sector risks; they are a bellwether, at best. Trying to aggregate the perception of corruption, money laundering risk, or sustainability is like aggregating crime across a large country. Your exposure is impacted by where precisely in the country, your attractiveness as a target, and your predictability. Do the bad guys know that you have excellent security and are not worth the hassle of hacking, or is your security framework implemented unevenly, with gaps vulnerable to exploitation?

Still confused? Don't worry. Risk assessment is the area – along with managing third parties – which baffles most people. Find me on LinkedIn; there are plenty more resources on my page, head to the Ethics Insight site for free risk assessment tools, or ask me a question.

These questions about your defences take us into the following assessment process, benchmarking your controls against the identified (potential) risks.

Benchmarking

Comparing yourself to others seldom ends well – we don't need to feel inferior or superior about our risk; we must feel cool-headed, with our eyes open, present, and paying attention. There is a lot of guidance – from those enforcing regulations – telling you what you should have in place. That's a good start, but it can be a bit overwhelming. Having done the hard work of assessing your internal culture and calibrating the external risk environment, now consider what you have in place to mitigate, manage, resist, or avoid those risks. If this is getting a bit technical, maybe Figure 2.1 will help.

We want to know your ability to prevent, detect, and respond to possible issues. Let's break that down.

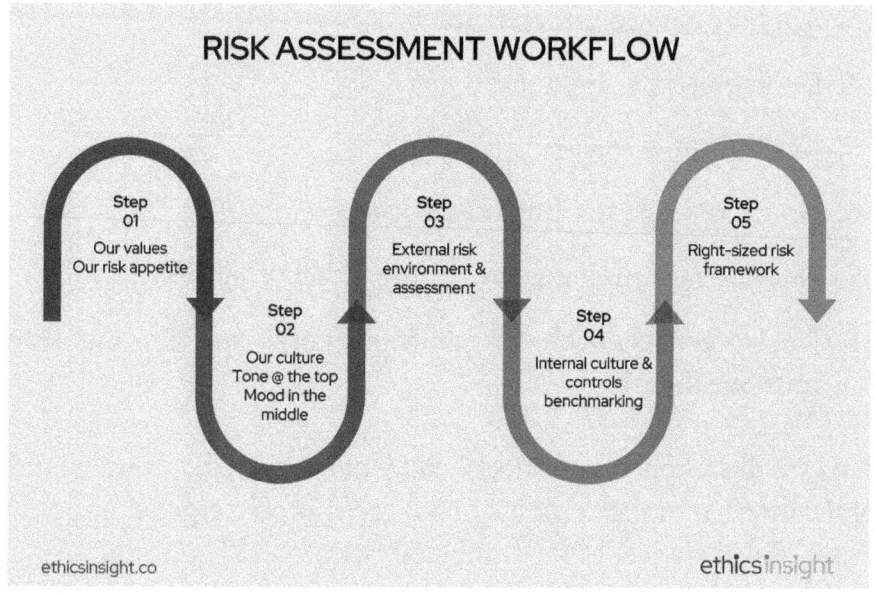

RISK ASSESSMENT WORKFLOW

Step 01
Our values
Our risk appetite

Step 02
Our culture
Tone @ the top
Mood in the middle

Step 03
External risk environment & assessment

Step 04
Internal culture & controls benchmarking

Step 05
Right-sized risk framework

ethicsinsight.co

ethicsinsight

Figure 2.1   Risk assessment workflow.

Prevent

Prevention is better than cure, they say. The trick here is to strike a balance between *having* and *doing*. Most organisations above a certain size will have policies, such as your website privacy policy. I'm more interested in what you do to make policies, frameworks, and rules jump from the screen into reality. Much of the remainder of this book will delve into specific risk issues, looking at how we can move stated intention into practical application. For now, though, look at your risk and compliance policies and procedures and ask a few questions, including:

1. Do we have any!?

2. Are they easy to access?

3. Are they easy to understand?

4. Do people refer to them?

5. Are they up to date?

6. Do we provide training on these topics?

7. Does this training involve testing (comprehension)?

8. Do we get feedback on our frameworks and continuously improve them?

This small sample of questions will get you started, but we would typically be more specific to make them more targeted and relevant. For instance, I like to include issue-specific questions – to understand how we address risk issues identified (in earlier steps) as appropriate to the organisation. For areas including corruption, sanctions, and human rights, it's imperative to assess the risk posed by people acting on our behalf. If you're using third parties, then you should include questions about any vendor (or equivalent) management processes, systems, and training you provide.

If you're stuck, head to our website – ethicsinsight.co – where we have various assessment tools.

Detect

Detection is straightforward – we want to know about your systems and processes to identify potential risk issues. What you do will have a significant impact here. For example, monitoring for potentially fraudulent (or otherwise suspicious) transactions should be part of the existing framework if you're a payments platform. If you're wondering what else to consider, break it down into what I might call transactional monitoring, people data, and security systems.

Transactions include the obvious financial ones, but we're also interested in the flow of anything of value through your business (people, counterparties, products, raw materials, waste, etc.). Using the output from your risk assessment will sharpen your focus. For instance, if you manufacture items using metals, monitoring the origin (for human rights and conflict issues) will hopefully be coupled with proper disposal and scrapping (a typical hotspot of fraud and organised criminal activity).

Do you know what your people think, feel, and do? That may seem strange, but if you're not capturing data from your colleagues – including where they perceive risk – you're driving your risk program without a map. You will likely already have employee surveys, exit interview processes, and appraisal data, but are you doing anything with that? If people are leaving a particular team, that might merit closer inspection. Conversely, if you never hear a peep from another department, is that a sign that all is okay, or are people fearful of speaking up? We will unpack speak up and monitoring in more detail, but please monitor whatever channels you use to listen to your people.

Information and physical security will invariably involve monitoring. Check if this extends beyond those two areas to include other possible risk issues. For example, do you conduct audits focused on these risk issues and monitor employee links with third parties? I am not suggesting Orwellian surveillance, but a data analytics query looking at employee and supplier bank accounts and address detail may uncover duplicates, meriting further scrutiny. It is a balance, but you have a right to some level of transparent and fair surveillance in your organisational home.

Respond

Response is not simply how you deal with potential violations; it's how you continue to operate, learn lessons, and improve. Yes, we want to know if you have an investigations framework, speak-up channels, and non-retaliation provisions. But we also want to know about business continuity and crisis management. If you're thinking, "What the hell is that?" don't worry. It's your Plan B. For example, if you suffer a data breach, where is data backed up and stored? How do you continue to operate? Or, how might you respond if you found a fraud involving your largest supplier (do you have a back-up)?

When you identify an issue, that is often just the start. Going back to our MRI analogy, you now know you must conduct further tests, including establishing the spread or impact on other organisational functions.

To benchmark your response framework, ask the following questions:

1. How do people raise concerns?

2. What is our investigative capacity?

3. How do we keep operating and minimise disruption?

4. How do we deal with uncooperative or hostile stakeholders?

If that last question sounds concerning, it's a reality. If you get hacked, don't count on large IT providers to prioritise helping you. Don't expect the police to bend over backwards to support you if you uncover a fraud. Suppose you receive a corrupt demand in a country where the rule of law cannot be relied on. Good luck getting the local authorities to investigate. These are all worst-case situations; hopefully, none will come to pass. You will need to be ready to continue operating without much support, so check if and how you can do that.

Getting the right blend of prevention (education and support) and detection (monitoring) may seem daunting, but it isn't once you have a right-sized framework to test *doing*, not just *having*. It will also help you work out what needs improving (hopefully) ahead of an issue.

Speaking Up, Non-Retaliation, and Consequences of Violations

Organisations with an effective speak-up culture typically detect issues more quickly, reducing financial, human, and operational costs. Having a speak-up framework is one of the simplest and most effective risk-reduction tools you can employ. To demonstrate the point, I built a speak-up channel on a surveying platform in an afternoon and confirmed that you do not need a 24/7 multilingual call centre to get started.

The Association of Certified Fraud Examiners' (ACFE) *Report to the Nations* includes detailed information, suggesting that median losses from fraud were typically doubled in organisations without hotlines. The average detection time was 12 months with and

18 months without a hotline.[2] The term hotline is a broad catchall for mechanisms whereby employees (and other stakeholders) can raise concerns (often anonymously).

If you're considering developing a speak-up framework, please check local regulations as they may include provisions on preserving anonymity, preventing retaliation, and statutory reporting requirements for certain offences. Once you're clear on what you must do, you may have a few decisions, including those summarised in Table 2.1.

Your next decision will determine who is covered by the reporting framework. Full-time employees, but what about contractors, temporary workers, business partners, third parties, customers, the local community, and whomever else might be impacted by your activities? The answer to this question will inform the choice of channel and tools. I would advocate for the more, the merrier – some estimates suggest up to half of the *tips* about wrongdoing emanate from outside your organisation.

Before communicating the reporting framework, anticipate one of the first questions, "What should we report?" Many reporting lines are misused, usually more misinformed than malicious. You will still get some "My boss is a douchebag" and "I didn't get the promotion I deserve" messages; that's pretty normal. It can help to have some sort of classification framework. You may not wish to publicise the entirety to all stakeholders, but it will help in subsequent phases, including investigations. A common catchall is "workplace misconduct", but I'm not a fan of that, as it's not immediately apparent to me (or most employees) what

Table 2.1 Questions to ask when you build a reporting framework

Question	Positive considera-tions	Possible downsides
Should we allow anonymous reports?	If people can report anonymously, you will get more reports and a potentially more accurate risk picture	Few reports include sufficient detail at the start, so having a mechanism to follow up with the reporter helps You will also have to filter out disgruntled or malicious allegations, increasing your workload
Which platform is best?	You know your organisation; choose the platform(s) that people use most. Ideally, provide options	Simple is best. It will be less effective if you have too many options or require too many steps for someone to make a report
In-house or outsourced?	Consider the capacity and resources you have. Can you respond to reports promptly internally? Do you have people manning the reporting channel 24/7 (allegations seldom happen at 9 a.m. on a Monday)?	Outsourced can sometimes mean requests to download apps or generate logins. Make sure the provider focuses on user experience. Consider how well you need and want the provider to know your business; do you need them just to record and pass on, or do some sort of analysis and triage?

constitutes misconduct (or why it needs to happen in a workplace to merit reporting)!

Your Code will help you identify the issues you encourage people to report. Be intentional, purposeful, and clear about the scope of the reporting framework; it will save a lot of time in the long run.

Once you're ready to socialise the reporting line, look at what else has worked. How do you communicate product or service updates (internally and externally)? Have you been through any particularly effective change programs or job-specific training? It is always easier to piggyback on initiatives that have worked rather than reinvent the wheel. As a tip, keep visuals simple. You will want a clear call to action (what, where, and how to report).

Test the reporting line periodically, ask people for feedback (and test knowledge during training and surveys), and monitor usage. Dig deeper if you see anomalies (e.g., two proximate departments with very different average reporting data). The reporting framework is not the sole or most reliable indicator of organisational health but can be a tremendous top-line indicator of high-risk areas within the organisation.

Investigations: What Do People Need to Know?

A robust speak-up culture is fundamental whether you use a speak-up line or not. Encouraging the lovely and intelligent people you work with to bring their best selves is a no-brainer. If you want your people to innovate, create, and make, you must allow them to um, err, and stumble. Earlier, we discussed questions to better calibrate the mood in the middle, including safety making mistakes, asking for help, and accountability. These areas are critical in a speak-up culture, distinct from call-out culture.

Publicly castigating others for perceived or actual violations is seldom constructive. Speak-up culture is different; it's more objective and grounded in the shared values, codes, and rules you collectively (as an organisation) agree to respect. For that to work, people need to trust your investigations framework. We must, therefore, work backwards to create a functioning and healthy culture where we can raise issues safely.

Let's start at the end of an investigation, where you decide what to do and to whom. Was the allegation proven accurate? Who is guilty, and to what extent (primary or accessory)? What is a fitting punishment? If you get this wrong, you lose trust, and people will stop speaking up. Let's use a case example.

Employees in a small manufacturer in a fast-growing emerging market (with a weak rule of law) are terrified of the boss. This leader has little appetite for opposition to her power. If anyone dares challenge her authority, she will invite them into her office and make various lurid threats (sometimes involving family and often with the pistol she keeps in her desk drawer, for emphasis). A brave soul has had enough and contacts the global head office one day. Guns and threats to family require sudden flapping and busy responses (with little forethought). A team of investigators flies in, but the boss knows they're coming (it's her factory, and no visitors get past without her approval). At the factory, the overseas team discover laptops wiped, sparkling and empty desks (free of sidearms), and serried ranks of cowed employees with little to say. Miraculously, and with some help, the investigative team find enough evidence to confirm the allegations. But the boss is also a director, and a significant local shareholder in the venture, with political connections that may thwart any attempted ouster.

For those of you tut-tutting that this wouldn't happen in your country (with a supposed strict rule of law), you're wrong. Baddies frequently get away with it. Sometimes on a technicality, sometimes investigative screw-up, in other cases, because they have leverage.

What's the moral of the story here? No one in your organisation can or should be irreplaceable if you have solid values and a healthy speak-up culture. In practice, this can be hugely challenging. The briefest glance at various Silicon Valley start-up scandals indicates that a powerful cabal (usually controlling most of the shares) at the top can spread toxicity throughout. Simply removing a majority shareholder is not simple at all! Still, it doesn't mean you shouldn't try just because it's hard.

What your stakeholders want from an investigative process is simple: trust. They want assurances that they will be protected and not subjected to retaliation if they speak up. Stakeholders want to feel the process is fair and transparent. I've seen many firms trip over that last bit, fearful about how much transparency is necessary. My view, as much as possible. Why? Three reasons; people talk, and if you think you can keep an investigation secret in this age of leaks and social media, you're in the minority. Get ahead of the story before it becomes the usual blend of stinky half-truths that squelch out of firmly clasped corporate cheeks. The second reason, you're robbing everyone of your best material. Failure is a much more faithful teacher than success; investigations must become case studies, training material, and honest discussions. Yes, we need to balance shame and disclosure, so for sensitive interpersonal issues (especially harassment and bullying), always seek consent and err on the side of less is more. But stories resonate for problems you will encounter again – unethical demands from external stakeholders to misuse of assets and property. I have trained thousands of people and always asked what was most helpful. The case studies within that organisation (sector or group) are the clear winner; a story paints hundreds of words of methodology and theory.

The third reason? Trust. By sharing (suitably shame-filtered) updates with your stakeholders, you trust them to handle the truth. Much like, as parents, we are told to discuss our failings and mistakes with our kids – including apologising – this trust removes some of the "them and us" piety in hierarchies.

So, what do employees need to know about the mechanics of your investigations? Not much. They don't need to know the intricacies of chains of custody (unless it's their belongings) or forensic imaging (unless it interrupts IT coverage). What stakeholders will want to know is:

1. Is it fair (justice for all)?

2. Will it be thorough (many investigations are not)?

3. Is it transparent?

4. Will you protect me if I come forward?

5. What do you need from and expect of me?

Communicate your position, and remember to avoid the dreaded *zero tolerance*. Explain that you will do your best, and then do it. Some investigations are inconclusive, especially when it is one person's word against another's. Your stakeholders will be unhappy in these cases, but they will respect the effort if you communicate transparently, deal fairly, and protect all those involved.

Investigations: How to (Not) Do Them

All those involved include the accused. The first mistake, especially in the social media age, is to forget the concept of innocent until proven otherwise. Everyone has the right to a fair trial and restorative justice (wherever possible). The second thing that happens when an allegation is made, or issue uncovered, is to assume that binge-watching crime drama transforms you into an (effective) detective by osmosis.

I was called to a meeting by an engineering firm in Singapore. They were involved in building infrastructure and would rotate hundreds of engineers in and out of the island. The company asked the head of Facilities Management to organise the serviced apartments for this conveyor belt of project workers. Some time later, the client identified payment anomalies in the invoices for these apartments; inflated payments, transfers during periods of no occupancy, duplicate invoices, etc. The facilities manager had his fingers in the till, with real estate agents in cahoots. The head of HR leapt into furious action.

She called the manager in for a meeting, seized his personal phone, recorded the session, and told him he'd brought shame to his family and, as the eldest, "Who will care for your parents now you're going to jail?" Shortly after leaving the meeting, the manager headed home, grabbed a hastily stuffed bag and fled the country.

Well, that went well. I wish this were an extreme example, but it isn't. Here's what your average person knows about investigations (Figure 2.2).

Seizing private property was not enough for our budding Jack Bauer; the HR manager proceeded to head to a dodgy phone shop and had the device jailbroken so she could read the messages.

Do not take private property and access personal data illegally; aside from the inadmissibility issue, breaking the law is generally not a sound investigative tactic. Don't record without checking it is legal and requiring the appropriate consent. Even then, ask, "Why are we recording? Does this further the cause and help

Figure 2.2 What most people know about investigations.

us secure our objective?" Recording can contaminate interviews (people's behaviour changes when recorded).

Avoid the temptation to shame. Your role as an interviewer (not interrogator) is to build rapport. When we feel empathy from the other person and connection, that might help us unburden our guilt. Guilt is directed at the act, and shame is directed at the self. Most people clam up when shamed. Even the most heinous offences may necessitate rapport and words like, "It was a mistake many others in your situation might have made." And, please, do not go in for the kill without a follow-up plan. What do you intend to do if you find guilt? Disciplinary action, dismissal, report them to the authorities? Understanding the objective will help plan when, how, and where to organise an interview.

Mind the Gaps

While I am confident you're not using the lousy cop, worse cop tactics, some of the less egregious pitfalls can still trip us up. A proper investigation could be (and is) the subject of many books in their entirety. I have much ground to cover and limited space. The first step is to step back. Don't get caught turning assumptions into *facts* and missing simple truths. Ask first, what do you *know* has happened? That might be a concise list, "Someone made an allegation that our CEO is misleading investors." Then list the assumptions and determine how you might test them. I like to use a *value* and *effort* matrix. Let's start with effort (or complexity), which is a constituent of:

1. **Context:** Local legal, political, and cultural dynamics (e.g., an allegation involving an influential stakeholder is more complex than one about a non-critical supplier).

2. **Access:** Can we obtain information? Can we speak to the reporter? Are those involved internal or external?

3. **Understanding:** Is this a familiar topic (e.g., theft of IT equipment vs ransomware from unknown threat actors)?

4. **Trust:** Do we have the reporter's trust? Can we consider their credibility (sadly, some allegations will be malicious)?

5. **Control:** If we find wrongdoing, can we do something about it (links to context, relationship dynamics, and leverage)?

It's not that you should discount assumptions if they're hard to prove. It's more about prioritising quick wins. Back in the mid-2000s, I was in China. At that time, most foreign firms needed a local partner. Occasionally that partner would steal the intellectual property and set up a parallel (counterfeit, close imitation) business. One of our clients feared this was the case. Determining ownership (on paper) of a nearby factory and gaining access to verify if they were (as suspected) producing rip-off products would have been challenging. Instead, we asked a potential client to call the factory and arrange a meeting. The client's business partner greeted our asset, handed over a business card, and explained he was the owner of the competing factory; assumption no more. There are usually a few ways to test a hypothesis.

What about the value? Taking a business card to the Chinese courts wouldn't have helped, especially without evidence that their business partner had handed it over and confirmed he owned the factory. This evidence had little value from a legal perspective. However, our client did not need that as they had little faith in the local legal system and wanted time to line up a replacement partner before terminating the relationship. The goal was to prove the suspicion with minimal fuss and limited risk of detection (snooping around records and factories is high risk). Therefore, in this case, the value and effort blend worked. In other cases, the value and effort thresholds can be much higher.

Consider what level of evidence you require to prove or disprove the allegation. If in doubt, get legal advice. Legal privilege and counsel are essential in some investigative situations, especially where you have to report regulatory infractions.

What Is Evidence?

Maybe it might help to place evidence on a scale, from the least robust to the more easily provable. We can't be exhaustive here, but let's focus on the evidence you'll most likely encounter.

First is anecdotal evidence, which cannot (typically) be used in court. Anecdotes are stories, and even if widely held, the danger is relying on *evidence* that may be hearsay, rumour, or confirmation bias. The saying, "No smoke without fire", fails to qualify that some tiny fires can create acrid and toxic smoke. Anecdotal evidence's best friend is character testimony. We now move from stories to what people feel about each other. Statements about someone's character can help if you're trying to understand the pressures people are under (that often precipitate ethical lapses) but be careful to sift out rumour, grudges, bias, and conspiracy.

Circumstantial evidence will be familiar to most, but let's ensure we're on the same page. Direct evidence is a witness confirming they saw John access the storeroom at 7 a.m. when we know that items were stolen from that location at precisely that time. Circumstantial evidence is a witness saying they saw John near the storeroom at 6.50 a.m. It's smokier and fierier than anecdotal but still treat it with the same rigour as when moving assumption to a fact.

Physical, material, or demonstrative evidence is what it says. For instance, CCTV recordings show John entering the stockroom at 7 a.m. Digital evidence might record John's biometric thumbprint entering the stockroom at 7 a.m. Digital evidence is frequently the organisational investigator's best friend – emails, messages, files, data, transactions, and anything else you can extract from digital devices. The overlap between physical and digital often occurs during the collection of publicly available data. For example, if you access corporate filings to show that John holds a competing business selling the same products as those stolen from your stockroom. Accessing that data may be digital, but the file may be a scan of a physically signed document (sometimes termed documentary evidence).

Don't worry about the differences; the critical point is to ensure that you appropriately record, preserve, account for, and record any movements (physical or electronic) of evidence. Deleting digital evidence is also (often) easier, so be careful there too. Do your research around the chain of custody considerations.

Digital evidence bleeds into forensics – specifically, and unsurprisingly, digital forensics! Other types of forensic evidence (fingerprints, blood, ballistics, and like) are rare in your common or garden variety of organisational investigation.

Phew! Let's assume you've gathered the evidence you might reasonably be required to. What now!?

Before You Start

When starting an investigation, resist the temptation to jump in. By now, you've hopefully got a clear idea about the objective and the limitations of data and evidence retrieval (for most of us). Let's instead focus on how you'll talk to people.

I know you've watched the TV shows and cannot wait to bust out your steely cop stare. No judgement. We've all been there. Maybe you even have a bright lamp and spent the day before yelling to rock classics, just so your voice has the right amount of rasp and gravitas. You get in early, set up the room with the jug of water and paper cups – you know that's a prop cops use when they need a dramatic pause in proceedings. The first suspect arrives. They ask you if you've got a cold and why there's an unplugged lamp on the conference room table (the cord didn't reach, did it?). Slightly rattled, you head for the dramatic pause water station and pour it on your crotch. Well, that didn't go as planned.

We get ahead of ourselves sometimes, and investigations get most people excitable. That's why we need PEACE. I'm not yelling; PEACE is an acronym for a model developed in the UK to reduce false confessions stemming from more aggressive interviewing techniques. PEACE is perfect for organisations where a non-confrontational conversation management process is always preferable. The five stages are:

P = planning and preparation
E = engage and explain
A = account
C = clarification and challenge
E = evaluation and closure.

Planning and Preparation

Fail to prepare, prepare to fail. When planning, ensure you've reviewed the case, the interviewees (suspects and witnesses), points to clarify or prove, the objective, and the evidence you have (and need). Now it's time to strategise. Some of the variables to consider might include the interview(s) location, recording protocols, interviewers' roles, and other considerations (e.g., translations, technology). We will also need to prepare both physically and mentally. Think about the presentation of materials – will you share evidence, and in what order? Check your own biases, get focused, calm, and ready to pay attention. Being fully present during an interview is draining, and there are plenty of distractions. I like breathing exercises beforehand to get centred and ready to pay deliberate attention. If I'm doing an in-person interview, I also like to have a few things in my investigator's grab bag (Figure 2.3).

Engage and Explain

Once the interview starts, that also has a timbre and tempo. Introduce the process – who is involved, housekeeping, timing, and like.

Figure 2.3 Contents of an investigator's grab bag.

Explain the purpose of the interviewee and who will be doing what. While you're doing this, observe the interviewee and establish their baseline. Now, the baseline may be tricky from the start, as few people walk into an investigation with a skip in their step. But your role is to try and put them at ease. Baseline is how we usually interact with others, mainly when dealing with questions or topics that aren't emotionally charged – name, job role, small talk. You want to use background details that aren't core to the event or issue to continue this calibration and rapport-building.

Check regularly to confirm the interviewee understands those ground rules. For example, "if anything is unclear, please ask", "don't leave anything out, but it is okay to forget". This process is good practice and allows you to check how the interviewee responds in the affirmative and negative.

Be honest to the extent you can. Yes, you may need to keep a few things up your sleeve, and you may need to use some deceptive lines of questioning. But, on the general purpose of the interviewee and the parameters, be honest. For example, don't make bad choices seem like a choice. You may antagonise the interviewee. If the guilty party likely faces some form of sanction – disciplinary, criminal, or something else – don't claim you can give them options when all roads lead to punishment.

The Account

Do you know someone who interrupts you frequently before explaining your points? How does that feel? Yeah, pretty crappy. Don't be that person.

Let the interviewee speak freely – sometimes called free recall. They may need some context to get started. Usually, it helps to take their memory to where you want them to start. Ask them to recall everything. Sometimes we filter out what we feel is irrelevant, but it may be salient for your investigation. Additionally, it's another behavioural cue.

Generally, true accounts are a bit messy. We jump around in timelines, correct ourselves, include superfluous details, describe interactions, and if you tried to draw the narrative, it would look like a spider on psychoactive substances. However, it is typically a linear progression when we manufacture a lie – like a straight train track. Lies often lack the details.

Your role as the interviewee gives their account is simple: listen and observe. Yes, one of you may be taking notes, but learn to do that while looking at the interviewee. You don't want to be glued to your notepad and missing crucial details. Please don't type unless it's a video call and you've muted your mic; it's frickin' distracting!

Once you have the first iteration of the account, ask the interviewee to expand on areas of interest. Use phrases like, "Could you go over the . . . again?" You are trying to gather a more fulsome picture, but this is also your chance to see if any non-verbal (or verbal) slips you spotted in round one occur again. Summarise to the interviewee to confirm you understand correctly and see how they react (sometimes we don't realise what we let slip). Let them correct, qualify, or emphasise topics you may not have understood. The simplest way to do this is reflecting and paraphrasing language – a potent tool to get people to open up, but you need to mirror the good bits!

Clarification and Challenge

There are no stupid questions, so the saying goes. There are, in fact, plenty of stupid questions. A brief tour of the YouTube rabbit hole confirms this. But, in an investigative setting, the only stupid questions demonstrate you didn't listen or prepare. That's why reflecting is so important – it encourages listening and creates rapport. Now is your chance to probe and clarify before closing the interview. Beware, however, that our memories like to fill in blanks, which can often be unhelpful in an interview setting.

During postgraduate studies in behavioural analysis and investigative interviewing, they asked for volunteers for a memory experiment. I put my hand up and soon had a blindfold and earphones as instructors led us around a conference venue and subjected us to disorientation, stress, and sensory overload tactics. The trainers warned us that the experience might not be pleasant. Our handlers bumped us around, screamed, and ran past us before shoving us into a room where they played bizarre sequences of sounds and music. The soundtrack was less whale song and spa muzak, more grenades and voodoo chants. The instructors handed us objects (still blindfolded) and gave us a few seconds to decipher what they were.

The purpose of this experiment was twofold – other students were able to quiz us (testing their interviewing skills), and we would compare recollections. It was sobering. Even data points as simple as the duration of sensory assault varied from 25 minutes to hours. The facilitators asked us to draw the route on a map; I was elated to get this bit right. I'd received training about counting steps and turns (right/left) in case of kidnap or detention. But that cognitive processing had seriously impacted other recollections. I thought a motorcycle air filter was a nasty 1970s lamp. A group of people, all primed and prepared for a mildly traumatic simulation, studying memory and behavioural analysis, were shockingly unreliable witnesses!

Were we an anomaly? No, our brain fills in the gaps, we assume, make logic leaps, and are not very good at remembering sequences or timelines. So many investigations rely on timelines, details, and descriptions. How should you manage this challenge? Gently take the interviewee back to the periods in their account that you need to clarify (for further details or inconsistencies). Ask them to set the scene, give them time, and jog their memory with any (non-revealing) evidence you might have. Be very careful if the event might be traumatic.

Don't just rely on a discussion. You can also ask people to demonstrate or illustrate if it clarifies the point (acknowledging some limits on remote communication). For example, ask the interviewee to draw or use items to mark where people and objects were. Think laterally; your role is to facilitate the interviewee's communication. Now is the time for empathy and rapport – yes, even if you think what the interviewee might have done is repulsive. You need to tap into their feelings, not their logical brain (busy filling in gaps). Why? Because we remember feelings better. Furthermore, we're much worse at faking feelings than we think – just recall the last present you gave someone that bombed!

If I asked you to recall a time when you (nearly) had a serious accident, would you accurately recount timelines, colours, and objects? Or would you remember sensations and feelings? Our emotions are (usually) a better vehicle to get us back to the location (and the truth).

We are sprinting through a topic that is more maze than a memo. Please don't rush to close and make sure you focus on the facts when summarising (not assumptions or sentiment). Closing is critical if recording the interview or gathering a written state-ment. Stick to the facts!

Once you close, explain to the interviewee what happens next (to the extent possible). Direct them to further support, especially in cases where a witness or victim (may have) experienced trauma.

Misbehaviour Analysis

"You missed a bit", the razor-brained among you might now be thinking. You glossed over clarifying inconsistencies. Yes, because it deserves its mini-section, although I could (and would love to write a whole book on this alone).

I am a behavioural analyst – I went back to study mid-way through my career as I recognised the importance of non-verbal cues and different investigative interviewing techniques. Teaching you about reading non-verbal cues is not for now, but questions or elements of an account that cause a deviation from a person's baseline are worth summarising. We must consider:

1. **The context:** Is the interviewee a suspect? Has the inter-viewee (possibly) suffered trauma? Are they speaking up against someone powerful? We must consider any contextual factor that might impact their emotional state.

2. **Consistency:** Are the emotional cues consistent with the story? Be careful here of *me theory*, where we think about how we might respond in each situation. The consistency we're looking for is a congruence between the substance of the account and the emotions conveyed. For example, if someone is saying how disgusted they were that anyone would steal

while smirking, that is interesting, and we might need to probe further.

3. **Baseline deviation:** We all have a natural way of communicating. Some of us are demonstrative and speak with our hands and body. Others are more monotone and reserved. Yes, the context can alter this baseline, but it's our job to calibrate the interviewee's *typical* behaviour and look for deviation from that. We do this with the standard questions you'd expect at the beginning of an interview (name, the purpose of the meeting, what their role encompasses, etc.). These introductions (and small talk, if appropriate) allow us to see how the interviewee responds to questions without a significant stake. A noticeable deviation might be a calm and collected type suddenly fidgeting, shifting in their seat, or seeming distracted and flustered.

4. **Spontaneity:** Is the account spontaneous and the responses similarly so? Don't confuse this with speed. Some of us might ponder questions and take our time making our points (our baseline), but we should still be coherent and spontaneous. A lack of spontaneity could be a fluent, confident, loud, and animated natural communicator suddenly stumbling, stuttering, going quiet, and repeating simple questions (to buy time to think of a reply).

5. **Cognition:** You know that moment when you ask a question and can almost see the other person's brain whirring, thinking? That's cognition, and we'd expect to see cognitive load (the amount of information the working memory can hold) if we're asking difficult questions. However, if you're asking simple questions (often recounting a supposedly lived

experience), that should not cause a significant burden on our working memory. We're looking for: (a) have we confused the person with any of our questions?; and (b) why they might need lots of brain processing power to ask this question. If there's no apparent reason, maybe brainpower is being deployed to fabricate a lie?

In other words, there is no one universal indicator of deception (or truth). Still, if we see significant changes in behaviour in particular parts of an account, that merits more examination. We're not concerned by one or two flickers. Deceptive indicators come in clusters across multiple channels in a short space of time.

What channels and what are the behavioural cues we're hoping to elicit? There are six:

1. **Face:** In particular, micro-expressions, and I strongly suggest you look into the work of Dr Paul Ekman[3] to learn more and practise your ability to spot them. I love micro-expressions and am forever indebted to my mentor Cliff Lansley and the team at The Emotional Intelligence Academy[4] in the UK, who took me under their wing and trained me to spot them. Micros are fantastic because they are impossible to fake (they occur in a fraction of a second), giving clues to our underlying and subconscious emotional state. They are universal (all humans, and some primates, exhibit micros). Micros occur across seven emotions – surprise, fear, anger, disgust, contempt, sadness, and happiness – and for an interviewer, they help you build rapport, be sensitive to the emotional stage of interviewees, and spot dissonance between what is

said and what the face tells us. Study them; it will be time well spent for every facet of your life.

2. **Body language:** Most written about, yet least universally reliable (so far). Much body language is culturally specific, for example, the head shake or nod. We're looking for inconsistency, a lack of spontaneity, body language occurring outside our presenting area (our upper torso and face), and deviations from baseline. Much is written about eyes looking this way or that and liars holding your gaze, but it's more about variation. For example, one of my kids usually is very animated, and their head bobs around as they speak, but when they're lying, the body is statue-like, and they fix you with a steely (hopefully convincing) stare!

3. **Pitch, tone, and volume:** Our voice also betrays our emotions. You will have heard phrases like "a curt tone" or "a depressed tone", which you'll associate with an emotional state. Watch to see how the music of our voice sings a different song. For example, does the pitch go down and quieten during sad elements of a story?

4. **Interaction style:** How does what the person says flow? Are they evasive or unclear? Do you feel like they're trying to manage your impression of them? Again, we all have our preferences and natural styles – and they will alter depending on the topic, our ego, and the context. Remember that a true story is lived and relayed as such. A lie is a fabrication which can impact clarity, flow, and impression.

5. **Verbal content:** Does what they say match the other behavioural cues and the context? Truthful accounts often resemble a plate of spaghetti. We jump around in the story, relate

elements that are not core, describe interactions between people, and self-correct, but there is a natural flow. Deceptive accounts are often linear – departing from point A and getting to point B quickly. In a truthful statement, you can ask us to jump back into the story wherever you like, and it's a lived experience, so we can. When we're asked to recount a fabrication, you might start to hear verbal slips (e.g., the wrong verb tense), stalling, and a drop in spontaneity and coherence. Watch out for distancing language – if it's something with negative implications (and we did it), we often want to put distance between us and the act or subject.

6. **Psychophysiology:** No, not the name of an experimental late-90s British electronic music band. Sweating, blushing, increased heart rate, hairs standing on end, and increased temperatures in legs (flight) or arms (fight) can all indicate changes in emotional states. However, it will be hard to detect with certainty in your average interview. So let's leave this one here unless you want to geek out – in which case, get in touch, and I can point you to some supercool research in this area, including evidence that most people in airports are angry (makes sense, right?!).

To elicit any of these behavioural clues, we must have good questions. There are many schools of thought on this topic. However, if it helps, I prefer to think of questions like a funnel. You start wide at the top, where the funnel is broadest, then narrow down as you need specificity and clarity. Something like this:

1. Tell me more about. . .

2. Take me back. . .

3. Walk me through. . .

4. Could you outline. . .?

5. Can you clarify. . .?

6. If I understood correctly. . .

7. What did you mean by. . .?

8. How. . . [explanation about the circumstances in which something occurred]?

9. What. . . [to get specificity about an occurrence, detail, or fact]?

10. Where. . .?

11. When. . .?

12. Why. . . [often accusatory and requires an opinion, justification, or explanation]?

You may wish to use tricky questions to try and catch someone if you think they're being deceitful, but be careful. Use these questions sparingly and only if you have a secure grounding (e.g., evidence the interviewee does not know you have). For example, a mind virus question is where you suggest you have information the interviewee does not know about. A mind virus question might start, "So there's no reason that someone saw you at that location?" Now the virus starts in their head, "What else do they know?"

Another common tricky question is a presumptive question, where you assume something and hope that exaggerating will prompt the interviewee to counter with a more reasonable confession. For instance, "We know you stole from petty cash on at least five occasions . . ." Here, you hope the person will confess to their lesser crime.

Be careful, if you're dealing with someone smart, they'll see you coming, and you'll have lost all the rapport and trust. I'd only use tricky questions if you have substantial evidence and are willing to have your bluff called.

The best advice I can give you to succeed in investigations is to use your ears and mouth in the ratio they were given to you. We all face that urge to jump in with that fascinating question, challenge or insight, but it's not about us. Our job as investigators is to gather data. It's hard to receive when you're on transmit.

Evaluate

Evaluating the interview is crucial. There is a tendency to rush or even overlook this stage. Sometimes, there is a bit of a cringe factor, especially if we must listen (or worse, watch) our performance. Have you ever heard a recording of your voice and said, "Oh, no, that's not how I sound, is it?" It's like that, but worse, because you'll inevitably realise you could've, would've, should've, asked better questions, or . . . shut up more! Just remember two things, no one cares as much as you do, and however badly it went, it will still be better than the "improv" my 15-year-old self put on at a school parents' day. As I typed that, my ears went red, my mouth pursed, and I inhaled sharply while groaning. No excuses then for not evaluating performance.

We're trying to understand what went well, how the roles worked, which interview objectives we met, and what needs improvement (including any corrective actions required). Self-critique first before seeking input from any co-interviewer (we're usually much meaner to ourselves; unless your co-interviewer is Dutch).

Once you've finished the self-flagellation – or putting your shoulder out patting yourself on the back – get back to the case! Review the information obtained (did you get what you needed?). Did you miss anything? If you receive further evidence, what will you do with it? Are there new avenues of enquiry?

I remember one particularly woeful internal investigation. High-value items (smartphones mainly) were disappearing at an alarming rate from a major online retailer's facility. The elite investigative team had spent the first week staring at the top of people's heads. They'd found CCTV footage, then assumed that the thefts occurred during packing for dispatch. The only problem with this foolproof assumption – assume, usually makes an ass of u and me – was that all packers wore disposable white caps and face masks. Team Clouseau had whittled down the suspect list from everybody who worked in packing to everybody who had a white hat or came near the packing station. Genius. It was revelatory when we elected to speak to a human (an oft-forgotten art in the era of screening pointless data). Each item has a code, and the code is scanned as the objects pass through the facility (arrival, quality control, storage, sorting, packing, dispatch). Each employee rotates through different parts of the plant, usually requiring swipe access to various locations and logins on the scanners. At this stage, data became useful, as we could look to see where coded items were dropping off the internal ether and who was on shift at those times. A pattern and small suspect list quickly emerged. Gathering evidence changes investigations.

Speaking to people – when you're prepared – changes investigations. Just make sure you properly evaluate and coordinate the next steps.

Learning from Failure

The excellent week-long hairnet CCTV staring meditation fiasco is a great lesson. You will fail in investigations. They are unforgiving as we deal with those pesky and unpredictable things: humans. Assuming the failure wasn't catastrophic (and it rarely is), see it for the lesson it is.

I told you about your ears and mouth ratio, and now I'll share the other great tip I received from a seasoned interviewer and investigator. Have hypotheses, as many as possible. I recently worked on an insurance claim – I know you're on the edge of your seat at the mention of the world's sexiest topic. A person had reportedly committed suicide in the States. The deceased's body had remained undiscovered for three months (until a welfare call from the building owner after neighbours complained of the stench). A registered firearm lay next to the body and an unregistered ammunition casing. Shortly after their death, a gentleman purporting to be a relative put in a claim for a huge life insurance policy, which had been upped by millions of dollars in the previous years, with no named beneficiary. The policy was issued in a country halfway around the world, and the relative was in a different country. What might have happened here? The possibilities and hypotheses are many. Who died? Was that their policy? Is the relative genuine? Why was there no-named beneficiary despite repeatedly upping the policy's value by $1 million? What was the relationship if they were a relative (given the body lay undisturbed for months)? Why buy a registered weapon and then seek illicit ammo? That's just for starters.

It's easy to make assumptions and leap to conclusions. But that's not our job. Our job is to seek the truth, discover the facts, and consider all the possibilities. Then, when we fail, to learn and come back better.

Endnotes

1. Cohen, P.A., Kulik, J.A., and Kulik, C.-L.C. Educational Outcomes of Tutoring: A Meta-analysis of Findings. *American Educational Research Journal*, 19(2) (1982): 237–248. doi:10.3102/00028312019002237.
2. https://www.acfe.com/rttn-archive.aspx
3. https://www.paulekman.com/
4. https://www.eiagroup.com/

3
RESPECT AND FAIRNESS

By now, we hopefully have a risk framework and at least the rudiments of a speak-up and investigative plan. We can use the risk data to frame what we expect of each other. There are few better places to begin than elucidating how we promise to treat people and the planet. During my career, I've seen various iterations of this – equal opportunities, affirmative action, sustainability, diversity, human rights, environmental and social impact.

Everyone said or says them. No organisations – at least that I'm aware of – publicly have confirmed their opposition to treating flora and fauna (including us) with respect and dignity. Environmental disasters came and went, animal testing continued, pay-offs (with non-disclosure strings attached) were made, and earning disparity persisted. Social media and the hashtag are now pushing the needle, and organisations are increasingly drawn into the debate around social and environmental issues.

I am summarising and skimming over vast swathes of (often Western-centric) social change and am aware that generational, demographic, and other factors have influenced the pressure for action, accountability, and transparency. I know these movements do not always travel globally, and this is a predominantly Northern European and US-led trend. I am also mindful that there are fringe elements on both sides that are malign and seek to obfuscate and castigate rather than meet any base threshold of evidential data. I am concerned by the ease with which someone can be *called out*, as it's frequently antithetical to the innocent until proven guilty maxim (and I have seen wrongful accusations).

But I am not here to disagree with the change because it's a constant. Yes, there will be bumps and pushback, but if we look at Victorian-era working conditions compared to today's workplaces, I think it's fair to bet on change.

We should instead decide on change. That doesn't mean a supine acquiescence to a sometimes-juvenile brand of university cod-Marxism espoused by mainly privileged kids. It means taking control of the topic and deciding what relationship we wish to have with people and the planet. It's an honest examination of our impact and efforts to reduce any harm we're causing others. Treating people and our environment with respect is a fantastic risk-reduction strategy. Unethical demands, threats, boycotts, and other nasty things are often fuelled by (perceived) inequity and poor treatment of environments and communities.

Where should you start? Maybe with your people. Diversity, equity, and inclusion (DE&I) is much discussed but often for the wrong reasons. It is, however, important in effective risk, ethics, and compliance frameworks and organisational cultures of integrity. Let's consider what it is, what we need to do, and how it helps manage risk.

Diversity, Equity, and Inclusion

What is it? Diversity is differences in backgrounds, character-istics, attributes, and skills. Equity is fairness; it is not treating everyone the same. It acknowledges that everyone has different needs, experiences, starting points, and opportunities. Inclusion ensures people feel they belong.

I am not a DE&I specialist. I come to this topic from the bro-ken side – seeing where cliques, inequity, and exclusion cause chaos. Therefore, this section is as much about what *not* to do as what to do. Which of the following words carry positive associa-tions for you?

- groupthink

- pack mentality

- exclusion

- intimidating

- unfair

- ignorant

- them 'n' us.

I could go on, but what do all those words have in common? They're words I've heard – and their synonyms – in many organisations struggling with integrity issues. These words are also indicative of cultures (often at the team of business-unit level) where differences were not tolerated. Cultures where one group dominates are easiest to corrupt, as they lack the coun-terbalance of divergent opinions. These groups might be bound by identity (race or sex, for example), but plenty of times, it's more complex.

Cognitive diversity (people outside the clique's groupthink) help counter this potential threat, but it's not viable if those other voices have no influence (equity). Inclusion (or belonging) occurs when we can speak up. Have you ever let a sexist, racist, or otherwise insensitive comment or aside pass unchallenged? Me too. If the statement came from a peer, we might assume you had some level of equity, but perhaps not inclusion. We can look the same as our peers but not be included. Each of us has felt like an outsider among people who may be externally similar.

In Chapter 2, I talked about speak-up culture as vital to a healthy organisation. Now, maybe you can see why DE&I matters. Without it, you're wasting the cash you spend on speak up, anti-discrimination, and anti-harassment initiatives. We must see each other as equals.

If you think this sounds a bit utopian, you're probably right. Humans appear to have an infinite capacity to marginalise the *other*. I get it if you're not a fan of identity politics – or at least its interpretation in many contexts. The movement creates some logic-stretches, not least, a simultaneous argument that we recognise each other as different and adapt accordingly, with the aim of being treated the same. Maybe we should focus on why DE&I matters for purely cynical organisational success – creativity and risk reduction. If we think and act homogeneously, we are not maximising the human potential of our people, and we're increasing the resentment that breeds risk. How might we do this?

Diversity

Let's unpack the sub-elements first. Diversity will differ from place to place. Diversity in Brazil and Canada differs from that in Japan or Papua New Guinea. These extreme examples indicate that a blanket policy is challenging, especially in globalised organisations. There may also be laws defining what has been termed protected characteristics (i.e., ones you cannot discriminate against).

Don't take a tick-box view with these lists. The easiest way to consider them – I have found – is to ask, "Do we look like our customers and communities?" If the answer is no, that is probably an issue – you might struggle to meet customer and community needs if you don't understand them. You will also increase your risk, as you can't relate to your constituents' pressures and rationalisations. Taking this objective snapshot is also pragmatic. For example, if your organisation is a not-for-profit focused on veteran affairs, it would not be unreasonable to have an over-representation (versus local demographic data) of veterans (and males). However, if you are a healthcare company focused on female fertility, your demographics would (should) be different.

Inclusion

> Diversity is being invited to the party. Inclusion is being asked to dance.
>
> Vernā Myers

Genuine and intentional diversity creates the space for innovation, creativity, and a better understanding of your stakeholders: this is inclusion. If your diversity policy is performative, that is not inclusion: it's cynicism. Performative diversity is stock images on many corporate brochures, where a smorgasbord of humanity feigns interest as they point at tables and charts or stare at screens. It's window-dressing for the most part, and we all know it. If you don't have the diversity of thought in decision-making (i.e., influential) roles, you might find you're on the wrong side of history. In the age of the internal leak, you may get away with it if everyone else is also doping in the duping Olympics but aim higher.

That's the negative risk reason for dodging inclusion. The more compelling risk management case is self-evident. If you want your people to speak up, help you identify issues, and develop clever solutions, you must make them feel welcomed, respected, supported, and valued. How you do this is simple in its complexity: listen, build trust, earn trust through action, learn, adapt, and improve. See, I told you, simple!

Equity

Why did I cite inclusion before equity if the acronym is DE&I? Because it makes more sense to me this way. As you move towards inclusion, we learn from each other, and the barriers to fair treatment, access, opportunities, and advancement become more apparent.

Let me use the example of international mobility. When I moved to Asia, the team I inherited was not Asian, at least not in any influential roles. We did not have a consistent level of understanding of our stakeholders. I am not saying that you must be Asian to understand Asia – some of the best analysts and investigators I know are non-native to the regions in which they excel. It's about balance. Hiring at senior levels in the local markets was challenging – as the industry was less mature in the region back then. Over the years, we implemented a hiring policy to reflect our communities better. I moved on to another internal role and watched as the team of those local talents left. Why? My friends explained that while they might progress in one regional office, they did not feel they'd have the same opportunities as we foreigners. For years, *talent* has been shipped from West to East, but a paltry trickle had migrated from East to West. There was little equity.

The elements of DE&I are iterative and complementary, not linear steps. To understand equity, we must often look at national, structural, institutional, and even geopolitical issues. If you think that's not me or us, it is. I recently interviewed a Malaysian financial crime expert. He is at the top of his game across Asia but wants to move to the US or the UK. Why then is he thinking of moving to Singapore first? He explained, "Good luck if you have a Malaysian guy trying to move from Malaysia to the UK. Even if it works, will I get the same salary as an expat moving back from Singapore?" The job is the same the world over, and his experiences across Asia would undoubtedly have substantial transferable value elsewhere. However, as I write, he's still in Malaysia.

We don't earn the same, and we don't have the same career opportunities. Yes, there are nuances to the argument – especially around preferences – but we need to make an effort to understand our people.

What Should We Do, Then?

Act on data you will (most likely) already have. Who do you employ, how do you employ them, and what do you pay them?

It is also about communicating data on your surveys – employee engagement, pulse, psychological safety, etc. If you're uncomfortable with that being shared or *leaking*, that makes sense; it's potentially invasive and subject to judgement by people who may not see the steps you're taking to address the current situation. However, is it worse than what's on Glassdoor (or your local equivalents)?

Transparency doesn't mean blurting out every bit of internal data; it is more about discussing the challenges and the DE&I journey openly and constructively. Openness is authenticity. I don't know about you, but I respect people, even if I (strongly) disagree with them if they are genuine and clear about their position. At least, in those cases, we can each make an informed decision. If your organisation is not about inclusivity, but hitting numbers and targets at all costs, say so. Plenty of people are willing to make that bargain.

Other tangible steps include recruiting, promotion, retention, and rewards. But I am no HR specialist. My skillset is often about finding problems, and errors, so I'll leave you with a few of the bigger stumbling blocks to effective DE&I:

- Keeping people on because they're "high performers", even if they're complete tools, creates toxic cultures that stifle inclusion (and diversity). Don't do that; it's a false economy.

- Bias training – it's a bit like writing with your non-dominant hand for an hour each year, unlikely to create much change.

- Relying on tech to "eliminate bias" – people build tech. That said, erasing name (and, if possible secondary school, which can be segregated by gender) data from applications isn't a bad start. However, proper testing and competency-based hiring practices would seem more promising.

- Cultural imperialism isn't always evil – the laws in many countries that actively encourage discrimination (especially religious) are worth challenging wherever you can. Don't hide behind shoddy local laws if they jar with your culture and values, especially if you have (economic or political) leverage.

DE&I is an evolving area, and we're making mistakes as we grow. Hence, I have way too few positive suggestions for you. Instead, I will rely on my mum's words, "There's always common ground to be found when meeting people one-on-one. It's when it becomes two-on-one that we can become such arseholes." If you're the two, try to be nice!

Human Rights

Well, this is a big topic, isn't it?! Human rights can comprise the following:

1. Corporate social responsibility

2. Community affairs

3. Social impact

4. Modern slavery

5. Indigenous rights

6. Supply chain transparency

7. Any proxy, pseudonym, or euphemism for the above.

Another way to phrase it: how you value the lives and livelihoods of those impacted by your activities.

This area has global-level guidance and regulation – including the United Nations' (UN) Guiding Principles on Business and Human Rights. We also have various national-level laws covering elements of human rights, including the UK and Australian Modern Slavery Acts, the California Transparency in Supply Chains Act, the Dutch Child Labour Due Diligence Law, and so on. Whenever I see this much legislation, unless the requirements differ widely (which they don't), the advice is generally, "Pick the highest bar as you'll always be covered." No one wants to aim for, "We use child labour and slavery in markets where we're allowed to."

Beyond laws, numerous non-governmental organisations (NGOs), the media, and civil society groups monitor the nexus between commerce and human rights. Employees, shareholders, and broader community stakeholders will also be scrutinising what you do.

Which Issues Are We Talking About?

The UN defines human rights as:

---

rights inherent to all human beings, regardless of race, sex, nationality, ethnicity, language, religion, or any other status. Human rights include the right to life and liberty, freedom from slavery and torture, freedom of opinion and expression, the right to work and education, and many more. Everyone is entitled to these rights, without discrimination.[1]

The Australian Modern Slavery Act 2018's list of offences includes:

- slavery

- servitude

- forced labour

- deceptive recruiting for labour or services

- forced marriage

- trafficking in persons

- domestic trafficking

- child trafficking

- debt bondage.

In simplest terms, if there is exploitation, that is a potential violation. Sectors that are particularly vulnerable are presented in Table 3.1.

Do's and Don'ts

Ignorance is no defence. You must understand the human rights and modern slavery risks to your business and supply chain. These issues cannot be outsourced to suppliers to manage. If you suspect, hear of, or identify possible/actual human rights violations, do not do the following:

- Act hastily.

- Push resolution onto your supplier.

- Try and conceal the issue.

- Outsource resolution solely to the relevant authorities.

The guidance accompanying the legislation and those from the UN and the Organisation for Economic Co-operation and Development (OECD) advice on Responsible Business Conduct is

Table 3.1 Vulnerable sectors

Sector	Possible issues
Resources (oil, gas, and mining)	• Environmental impacts on local communities • Worker welfare, including the use of migrant and/or low-skilled labour
Agriculture	• Land rights and land use • Environmental impacts • Worker welfare, forced labour, and child labour
Infrastructure	• Land rights and land use • Environmental impacts • Worker welfare and forced labour
Manufacturing	• Worker welfare (including working with hazardous substances), forced labour, and child labour
Information technology	• Governments requesting censorship • Governments requesting information sharing on users (especially opposition and dissidents)
Business process outsourcing	• Worker welfare (including working conditions and stress from content or customers)
Institutional investors	• The issues mentioned above when investing in these sectors

detailed and includes sector-specific considerations.[2] The consistent themes include:

- **Risk-based assessments:** A one-size-fits-all approach will not work. Assess the risk factors in your supplier base, including:
  - their sector;
  - their location(s) (resources including the Global Slavery Index provide country-specific risk information);
  - if they source from other regions or sectors;
  - thinking not in terms of risks to your organisation but dangers to people.
- **Support your suppliers:** The levels of understanding around human rights issues and how to manage them will differ:
  - Work with suppliers to **improve their awareness and response**. You are jointly responsible for assessing and addressing human rights and modern slavery risks.
  - Discuss with suppliers what to do if they **suspect or identify a potential issue** and explain the consequences for not doing so (including termination). Given the commonality of the term "zero tolerance", avoid it or clarify that it refers to failures to escalate possible issues, not for identifying problems, in case suppliers are scared to share information.
  - Try and **lighten the supplier's burden**. For example, if multiple other customers audit the supplier, suggest mutual recognition of audits, or push for industry standards.

- To save time and resources, add human rights to **existing checks** you conduct on suppliers (e.g., workplace health and safety, prequalification, and tendering).

- **Use your leverage for good:** Think about how your decisions may impact human rights risks:

  - **Do not unduly pressurise** your suppliers on costs and time-frames that may be unsustainable without exploiting workers or their suppliers.

  - **Be realistic** about how quickly suppliers (given differing resources) may implement adequate risk controls and support them where possible.

  - **Focus on suppliers with influence** in their supply chain (e.g., suppliers assembling products from multiple sub-suppliers).

- **Respond and report honestly and transparently:** The Australian legislation encourages organisations to report on their efforts to mitigate modern slavery risks. NGOs and civil society are increasingly pushing for similar transparency.

  - **Seek help:** Acting too fast may further harm the victims. Get professional support and advice from the government and trusted partners.

  - **Focus on resolution, not guilt:** Terminating a supplier may be the quickest option, but that does not help the victims. Focus on the best interests of the victims when seeking to resolve issues, including in decisions about ending relationships with suppliers. Consider if the supplier is unable or unwilling to address the problems.

- **Investigate cautiously:** Often, the initial suspicion, allegation, or suggestion of a violation will lack detail. There can be severe consequences for those making claims, so be cautious in any investigation and intelligence gathering.

- **Think before involving local law enforcement:** Consider if you can trust the judicial process, investigating agencies, and other relevant authorities in the country where the alleged violation occurred. Sadly, often the answer will be "no", and worse, they may be complicit. In these situations, get professional advice (including government affairs) to ensure the safety of the victims is the primary focus.

- **If you have contributed, own it:** Take responsibility for any contribution to suffering and cooperate fully in the remediation. After responding to the initial issue, consider working with civil society and reputable international and national organisations that may help prevent reoccurrence.

Discrimination and Harassment

Have you ever worked for (or lived with) someone abusive, harassing, and marginalising? Did you feel loyalty to that person – a desire to go above and beyond? Didn't think so. Organisations that tolerate discrimination and harassment will face increased risks, notably suboptimal performance, high(er) turnover, and in my anecdotal experience, more integrity issues and fraud (and other criminal activity).

If leaders – or the majority group – can treat people poorly with minimal sanctions, why would they stop there? Think of the

Silicon Valley unicorns with *bro* cultures. They condoned bullying and extreme pressure that led to corruption, human rights abuses, securities fraud, and other regulatory disasters.

HR typically manages discrimination and harassment, usually badly. If you are a risk, ethics, and compliance officer, at the very least, you might want to ask HR to keep you in the loop – it's your best early-warning indicator of problems to come.

How to Manage the Issue on a Global Scale

What is considered discriminatory varies widely across the globe. Pick a best practice standard, but be mindful that it may not be enforceable in the local courts should you want to act against employees. For guidance, we again look to the States, where the focus is on characteristics, including:

- race
- ethnicity
- nation of origin
- gender
- gender identity
- religion
- sexual orientation
- marital status
- age

- disability

- family responsibilities

- political affiliation.

Discrimination can be direct – for example, in recruitment, conditions of employment, denial of opportunities, progression and rewards, and unfair dismissal – or indirect. Indirect discrimination occurs when a policy or condition of employment seems to treat all employees the same but unfairly disadvantages someone because of their characteristics; for example, a requirement of 12-hour shifts that may not be possible for those with family commitments.

There are different local definitions of harassment, but I've used a standard one: "Behaviour that causes mental or emotional suffering, which includes repeated unwanted contact without a reasonable purpose, insults, threats, touching, or offensive language."

Do's and Don'ts

Don't tacitly or actively tolerate any of the following:

- Discrimination or harassment of an individual based on an attribute or characteristic.

- Any form of humiliating or unfair treatment.

- Belittling or humiliating colleagues or making or communicating derogatory comments, insults, or jokes that target a particular group.

The leadership must set the standards of expected behaviour by treating each other and all employees with dignity and respect. The organisation's values cannot live on paper; they must be adhered to at every level, including disciplining or removing powerful or successful people.

Organisations will often look to training to reduce the risks of discrimination and harassment. Having sat through conscious/unconscious bias and sensitivity training, I don't think it works. It's a bit like going to a hypnotherapist for one session in the hopes you'll cure that phobia you've had since childhood. Reducing discrimination and harassment may be better served by measuring psychological safety and starting the long journey of self-reflection. If you think that sounds glib, here's a story that brought home the disjoint between our perception and reality.

Two co-founders – one of South Asian and the other of North-East Asia heritage – built their business on a bedrock of inclusivity and tolerance, or so they thought. Scarred by experiences of discrimination and harassment in previous roles, the founders were very proud of the diversity and culture. That was until they saw the results of a psychological safety survey. The results indicated that the founders' particular brand of anti-discrimination was focused on their experiences and did not consider their workforce. No one felt safe discussing discrimination or any dissenting views on the topic, as the owners had created a brand of thought theocracy.

We can't build effective anti-discrimination and anti-harassment frameworks until we collectively understand what that means within our organisation. In other words, listen.

Non-Retaliation

Protecting those who speak up or speak out from retaliation is essential. After discussing investigations, I'd typically introduce this topic, but it sits naturally next to harassment. Unfortunately, many of those speaking up suffer for it. This retaliation usually occurs after someone:

- reports what they believe in good faith to be discrimination, harassment, or a violation of policies or the law;

- expresses intent to report what they believe to be a violation;

- assists another employee in making a report;

- participates in an investigation, audit or equivalent.

Retaliation can take many forms, including:

- terminating employment or assignment;

- intimidation or threats, implied or direct;

- excluding the person raising the concern or complaint;

- pressuring someone to drop or not support the issue raised;

- confronting (or disciplining) the complainant;

- providing a poor performance evaluation of that person;

- removing the person from their current duties or assignments;

- adversely altering the duties or work environment of the person raising the concern (including interfering with their career development opportunities).

You'll probably now be thinking, how do you prove retaliation? It's often hard. The most common threshold I've seen is, "Would a reasonable person think the (in)action was retaliation?" There are a lot of assumptions and context needed to arrive at reasonableness. I'm not suggesting that it has no merit, but if your organisation has effective (comprehensive) career and performance management frameworks, a deviation from that path is easier to spot. But what if an under-performer reports a violation? There's no magic answer, but one of the more promising trends I've seen is appointing a case officer for each person making a report.

The case officer must sit outside of the teams involved. They also need to have had significant line management experience to help determine whether alterations in working conditions suggest retaliation. Finally, this point of contact must have a clean record themselves!

Whichever structure and thresholds you adopt, communicate them clearly and often. When retaliation does happen, respond decisively. In some organisations, you may be blessed with a culture where bystanders call out bullying and retaliation. But most of us still need to rely on solid enforcement and messaging. Just think back to school; the teachers policed playgrounds and classrooms for a reason. Your leadership must be similarly visible and decisive when spotting bullies – in practice, especially in the remote era and with large, decentralised organisations, it is challenging. Make sure the messaging regarding your speak-up line covers non-retaliation.

Security and HSE (Health, Safety & Environment)

Security alone, let alone when coupled with HSE, is worthy of a book (or 20) on its own. My job here is not to break down what you need to do in each area but to explain where they interface with integrity risks and what lessons we can learn.

Security

Integrity issues bleed into security problems in many of the markets I work. Extortive requests – usually from public officials – often carry the threat of harm (or at least denial of liberty). Business partners (or employees) retaliate (physically or in the virtual realm) when you end relationships. Non-state actors (including armed militias and terrorists) demand revolutionary taxes or else. State-sponsored criminals use social engineering and weaknesses in your information security to steal, collude, violate data laws, and more. Regulatory authorities strong-arm your employees during dawn raids, taking data and equipment they shouldn't. I'll leave that happy list there for now, but you get the point.

What's the solution? Pretty simple, thankfully: ensure your risk assessment includes contingency planning and scenarios for high-stakes decisions. For example, if you know a particular government stakeholder (often the police or military) likes to detain or threaten your colleagues, work with security on ways to manage, mitigate, avoid, or transfer that risk. Good security risk management is intelligence-led, and we in ethics and compliance can learn much from this approach. Understand who's who in your neighbourhood and then consider the threat they may pose. The easiest way to calibrate a threat is to consider intention and capability. Past actions by critical stakeholders will often give clues as to their intention – for police officers, armed groups, or state-sponsored spies; this isn't their first rodeo. We tend to overstate capability and assume threats to be credible. While this caution is generally wise, do test those assumptions, remembering that everything these antagonists are doing is probably illegal under their laws!

Work with security to train your people properly. Few of us instinctively respond well to threats of harm or detention. Hostile environment training, crisis management simulations, and dawn raid protocols will be staples in a good security team. If you don't have one, this is an area to have a phone-a-friend capacity (a security consultant you can access immediately). Some insurance policies now offer this, especially for cyber incidents.

If you think I'm exaggerating this risk, speak to your colleagues in frontline markets. I remember working with an American company in Malaysia. They discovered a collusive relationship between employees and suppliers (a long-running fraud). The company duly fired those involved. The following day the local manager who had managed the dismissals was attacked with a Parang (a large knife), and the wife of the American country manager was beaten savagely outside their children's school. Conservatively, I've observed a security component to compliance issues in approximately 40% of the investigations I've worked on across Southeast Asia (the percentage is consistent with prior experience in other regions).

Security professionals are (typically) good at thinking in scenarios and percentages. This approach to risk estimation is constructive as it forces us to consider knock-on impacts and alternative scenarios. I use one particular crisis management framework for many other risk considerations. It goes something like:

1. What are the facts? There will often be very few facts; that's fine. That's what the next step is for.

2. Don't make decisions based on assumptions; test them. If the conundrum – a dilemma, an unethical demand, or a possible issue – includes assumptions (as they usually do), which of those can be tested? Just because someone claims something doesn't mean it is accurate or will happen.

3. Having tested assumptions, what scenarios shall we consider? Rank them by probability (in percentage terms) and give them names (best case, worst case, outlier, most likely, etc.).

4. Who do we need to inform (about the scenarios and their consequences), and whose support do we need?

This simplification of a process that can be very involved provides rigour and the opportunity to seek multiple inputs. Often, in some high-stakes situations, we need varied perspectives. The need is more acute if your leadership team are prone to groupthink – a bunch of Type A, high-level thinking optimists are not your best bet in a crisis.

The other area we can learn from security folks is deterrents and controls. If I asked you to think about a secure building and sketch it, it would look different from another reader's drawing living in a different environment. Yet, in ethics and compliance, we see people default to the same old guidance – usually issued by the US regulatory agencies – without first considering what you do, where, how, and with whom. A downtown office for a law firm specialising in patents and intellectual property presents a very different security problem to a construction site at a remote industrial park.

The security mindset will consider, among other things, your ability to do the following:

1. Prevent (secure access, perimeters, deterrent measures, etc.).

2. Detect (diagnostics, monitoring, alerts, etc.).

3. Respond (rally points, communications, crisis simulation training, etc.).

The prevent, detect, and respond mantra works well in all risk areas. It can help us step back from the morass of lengthy guidance. What in our framework helps with prevention, prediction, or response? Are we paying enough attention to each element?

HSE

Poor decisions can have severe health, safety, and environmental impacts. There are many lessons HSE can teach us in ethics, risk, and compliance.

Have you ever had an accident? No, I'm not about to sell you insurance or an ambulance-chasing law firm's service. If you cast your mind back, did distraction, fatigue, or rushing contribute? HSE experts understand that we must consider distraction and decision fatigue. Many compliance folks especially could do well to consider this. The answer to every compliance challenge is not more questions, forms, or processes. Often that will lead to the opposite outcome.

What about rushing, then? The next area an HSE accident-spotter will consider might be pressure. When time and budget are factors, we cut corners. Do you know where your people are under stress? Clues to help whittle down the employee dataset include areas with "ambitious targets", high turnover or a preponderance of newer colleagues, and poorly understood business areas. If you don't know what the "service excellence delivery" team does, nobody else will, including management. Therefore, this team may be throwing tennis balls against the wall and finessing their word search skills, but they may also be doing crazy dangerous stuff. Check it out.

You will have heard of environmental (and social) impact assessments. The good HSE professionals speak this. Maybe we should consider governance or integrity impact assessments? Environmental experts will tell you about the environmental costs of manufacturing photovoltaic cells or tidal energy generation systems' (in)efficiency. Why do we not subject all the new-fangled ethics and compliance technology, initiatives, and ideas to the same impact analysis? For example, in many organisations managing third parties used to be led by the group needing the product or service. To *drive efficiencies*, we created procurement teams. The rationale may have seemed sensible – especially if hiring managers had their hands in the supplier's cookie jar – but it doesn't always work. It can be challenging for a team usually centralised in one location to understand the local context, needs, and customs adequately. Just because everyone else does it, you don't have to!

Finally, on this whistle-stop tour of a HUGE area, I'd like you to consider British road safety. If you've made it this far in the book, I hope that last sentence doesn't prompt you to think, "I knew I should have used this to start a fire, especially given energy costs." According to varied (and searchable) agencies, the UK has some of the safest roads in the world. How has a nation whose hobbies have traditionally included binge drinking, hooliganism, and invading others achieved this? The feat is remarkable when compared to other countries with similar populations and significantly better infrastructure.

I noticed a few things on a recent trip across the South of the UK:

1. We saw variable speed cameras on large motorways where people gun it (measuring average speed). Technology solutions can live in situations where we rush, like data analytics monitoring expenses or third-party payments.

2. On sweeping roads with panoramic views across the countryside, messages saying, "You're entering a high-risk area, take care." Where distractions and overconfidence abound, remind people.

3. On hilly and snaking passages, before you hit sharp corners, they give messages about max speeds you can safely take the next corner. In trouble hotspots, provide clear information (numeric) around when it's safe to proceed.

4. As we neared Devon (a popular escape spot for city folks across the UK), we saw messages that "tiredness kills" immediately before the service stations/rest areas. We must understand where (decision) fatigue and pressure compromise ethics in your business and then message accordingly.

5. The messages change (using LED signage). These changes help overcome the situation where we ignore advice as we think we know it (when did you last watch the aviation safety briefing?).

These cues and tactics are all HSE at its finest and a sobering lesson for other parts of risk who remain verbose in the extreme of barely literate. If you can communicate the right message, using the right mediums, at the right time, you're winning.

Endnotes

1. https://www.un.org/en/global-issues/human-rights
2. https://www.oecd.org/industry/inv/responsible-business-conduct-and-human-rights.htm

4
CONFLICT-FREE ZONE

We're not trying to solve world peace. We're talking about where our activities or interests might clash with an employer's.

Conflicts of interest – as the name might suggest – are areas where the interests of two parties differ. In an organisational setting, the most common hotspots involve situations where:

- The organisation's interests differ from the interests of a client or business partner.

- A colleague's personal, family[1] or financial interests compete with those of their employer, a client or business partner.

- The organisation cannot act in one client's best interest without negatively impacting another.

Why devote a whole chapter to this topic? Because, in my experience, it is an issue in every single organisation, no matter the size, scope, or location. I'm not suggesting that we are all out to exploit our employers or clients; it's a very natural and human problem.

Let me give you an example. Years ago, after a slew of complex crisis response cases – death, mayhem, extortion, and a Manila hotel which streamed live CCTV footage of the reception desk on the in-room TV (strangely hypnotic) – I was relieved to get a project in New Zealand. If you've not been to New Zealand, imagine the most beautiful place, with polite people. It's unnerving, especially for those of us from countries with legendarily lousy customer service. Bewildered by an immigration official who asked about my job and jokingly said, "Welcome to Wellington, Mr Bond," I arrived at the hotel. The receptionist was so kind and interested to hear about my trip that I was suspicious. An Australian colleague leant over and said, "It's not sinister; they're just unnaturally nice here." Unnaturally was a superb and revealing word choice.

We were in Wellington to run ethics & compliance risk assessment workshops for a heavy equipment manufacturer. Usually, the arrival of "The fun police", or "bore patrol", as you get accustomed to being called, is heralded with that same low sighing exhale of breath my daughter does when I ask her not to leave toenail clippings on the dining table. Not in New Zealand. Our hosts had adorned the reception with a massive welcome sign, and we were offered refreshments (and this time, I didn't fear that they'd been stirred with the nose-picking finger).

When we started the workshop – often a sea of folded arms and daggered stares – it was like primary school on those days at the end of term where the teacher can't be bothered and lets you watch a movie. A palpable air of excitement hung unfamiliarly in the conference room. Before we could utter a word, a bright spark stood up and said, "We've worked at [out] our buggist [biggest] rusk [risk]." [I'm sorry, I can't resist phonetic Kiwi transcription.] They continued, "You see, we have 11 sites across NZ, and the smallest is in a town of 10,000 people. So if we don't employ someone's relative or whatnot, we wouldn't be able to work. What should we do?"

The lesson is that conflicts of interest need not be a problem if we're open about where work meets the reality of our life outside work. Let's break it down into issues and solutions.

Outside Employment and Side-Hustles

Many employees are dissatisfied with their job. Is it any wonder that people consider alternatives? Other factors might lead us to look for additional roles and side-hustles.

The remote working era freed time in many people's calendars. Gone was the brutal commute, inane meetings (without mic/cam mute options), watercooler gossip, and "Have you got a minute?" timewaster chats. What to do with all this time? Once YouTube rabbit-holes and streaming binges became as spirit-crushing as meetings, we emerged with new hobbies, fitness routines, reading time, sourdough recipes, or additional work (employed or self-generated).

For others, the needs are more urgent – money. We might need more money for many reasons, not least rising living costs. It might also be that you just want to try being your own boss or start that company you always dreamed of. I can relate to that! Whatever the reason, we must have a mature and pragmatic approach to managing these issues. Let's look at some examples I've come across recently.

1. The software developer who took a role at one big tech firm found it so easy that he took another job at a second tech giant.

2. The lawyer who advises start-ups on the side and sits on the advisory board of a few more.

3. The mechanic who works for their employer's clients, fixing machines out of hours and on weekends.

4. The consultant who takes time off work to run workshops (paid) unrelated to their job.

5. The procurement specialist who uses her sourcing expertise to help a relative's catering business whenever she's free.

Three of these people were fired by their employers – 1, 3, and 5. I was person 4. A good friend is person 2. Was that fair? Let's break it down further.

The software developer signed a contract saying they'd devote their time exclusively to both employers – a tough act. While not competing in the same consumer space, the tech companies competed for broader tech talent and investor dollars. Could the developer have told his employer, "Hey, this is really easy; if you pay me double, I'll do twice as much work"? Sure. Would they have done it? No. While I admire this person's industry and commitment, they did sign *two* contracts binding them to semi-competitive entities. Therefore, the issue here relates to contractual duties and not working with competitors – the latter may be a more compelling conflict of interest. Could his knowledge gleaned at Company A, on their dollar, have benefited Company B? Yes = conflict.

In case 2, my friend sought permission and explained that the start-ups he was advising worked in wholly non-competitive areas to his employer. He got approval for each role and gave up his evenings, weekends, and days off to get work done. His employer judged that his duty to them was not negatively impacted, and there was no conflict between a day job in a manufacturing firm and weekend work with diversity-focused tech start-ups.

In case 3, it's messy. The employer created rules that precluded them from supporting their clients out of hours. But sometimes machines break at inconvenient times, and there's an urgency – in this case, infrastructure projects are often done overnight to minimise disruption (roads, railways, etc.). The problem is the employer could argue that the mechanic was taking income that might come to them – albeit from a pissed-off customer who's been awake all night and had to wait for you to rock up at 9 a.m. The mechanic did not offer his services (overtime) to his employer to do this work at his inconvenience. It is a conflict to take money from the hand that feeds you and not tell them.

In case 4, I'd spent years doing further study on my own time and budget and love running deception detection and investigative interviewing workshops. I asked my boss if I could take time off work to run these and explained that I'd be paid. He agreed. My employer could have decided such workshops were within their scope – as they did provide investigations – but luckily for me, they hadn't gotten around to it – a slightly grey area of no conflict, saved by disclosure.

For the procurement specialist, her firing was unfortunate. Her job was frighteningly dull and easy for her. So when she wasn't buying widgets, she was on her phone helping out with the catering enterprise. Her undoing was not disclosing the side-hustle and a relatively strict interpretation of "when you're at work, we own you, even if we're too witless to utilise you properly". Furthermore, she used company stationery (to print flyers), which was unwise. Honestly, though, I've worked at some elite dipshit companies where people spend their days reading newspapers, playing on their phones, "nipping out for coffee", online shopping, and running their property rental business (which strangely always seems okay), etc. The lesson, I think, will not be music to the compliance purists: buy a printer.

In conclusion, there are some hard lines and some wiggly ones that might look like:

1. **Hard line:** If you're hired to do a job you're not fulfilling.

2. **Hard line:** If you don't disclose, you have issues.

3. **Hard line:** If you have access to competitive information, don't use it to benefit anyone else.

4. **Hard line:** If you're taking money from your employer, you're in trouble.

5. **Wiggly line:** If someone is underutilised, that's not always their fault.

6. **Wiggly line:** If they're doing it on their own time and it's not a hard line, do we need to play hardball?

7. **Wiggly line**: If our inefficiency has created a market opportunity we won't/can't exploit, shouldn't we step back and look again?

It should become more manageable if we link back to values (avoiding Purpass). For example, if your organisation is about breaking boundaries and innovation, you may need to provide avenues for hyper-productive employees to overachieve (incubators, internal start-ups, etc.). If, however, you provide heavy machinery, which (if misused) can injure or kill people, your values might link more to trust, reliability, durability, or resilience. In those cases, it's easier to evidence how unsupervised out-of-hours maintenance of *your* equipment could impact reliability and trust.

Friends and Family Discounts, Dismissal or Disclosure

Thankfully, managing friends and family conflicts is less complex than those in the previous section. In the example above with the affable Kiwis, disclosure is the key. But first, let's see how it can get messy using a few recent (and non-exhaustive) examples:

1. Your sister-in-law asks you to put in a good word for your nephew, who has applied for a role with your employer.

2. A good friend works for a customer and asks for *mate's rates*.

3. You start a romantic relationship with a colleague.

4. You were an early-stage investor in a relative's business. That company is now tendering for projects with your employer.

5. Your employer is the primary source of income in a small town, and some of your relatives' companies provide services to the firm. You work in procurement.

In most cases, you are passive; you are not initiating anything (except for the romantic relationship). So why might you be the source of a conflict of interest? Because disclosure is paramount. Let's play out those examples in some sort of worst-case and then best-case scenarios as they should provide a roadmap to avoid these (all-too-common) issues.

Nightmare Nephew

You tell the hiring team that your nephew is amazing without disclosing your familial relationship or that he's had a tough time of late (perhaps a scrape with the law). You say that a friend knows them well or works with them. Your employer duly hires the kid. Your nephew joins a slightly dysfunctional team with an absent manager and quickly becomes demotivated and confused about what he's meant to do. He is later busted for stealing from the company. During his performance reviews and disciplinary hearings, he says, "But my aunt never told me this job would suck so bad." Your employer fires you for not disclosing your relationship and bringing a fraudster into the firm, doh!

OR

You disclose to the hiring team that your nephew has applied for a role. You explain that you've not worked with him, and he's had difficulty turning his life around. You suggest that if your employer hires him, he will benefit from close hand-holding to build up his confidence with a hands-on and emotional astute manager (or mentor), but he was very loyal as a kid. Your employer has a program to help reintegrate past offenders back into society. They decide to proceed with the hire. Your nephew grows in confidence thanks to a skilful and attentive mentor. He wins employee of the month, and your family thank you profusely.

With Mates Like These

You consent to the demand for a discount. Your *mate* changes the terms of the engagement, makes routine out-of-scope requests, and pays late (or never). After a while, someone sharp-eyed in finance starts asking questions about this floundering and unprofitable project. A colleague, unbeknownst to you, spills the beans and says, "I have no idea why we took on these clowns; I think the client contact is a mate of Derek" [yes, you are now called Derek]. You are called into a meeting and fail to disclose the friendship. Your employee suspects you're in on a fraudulent kickback scam with the hopeless client, and they suspend you to investigate the matter.

OR

You explain to your *mate* that it may cost you your job if you discount. They decry your unwillingness to "be a proper mate [by risking your job]". You realise they are hopeless and decide you deserve better mates.

Staff-Crossed Lovers

You sneak around, confident that all humans around now have vastly inhibited senses of perception and don't notice the furtive glances, brief touches, overfamiliar sharing of food, and text giggles. Resentment in the team grows as (rightly or wrongly) they perceive your blossoming romance is unfair; perhaps one of you is in a position to aid the other's career (a supervisor, maybe). Eventually, a hacked-off colleague calls HR or the whistle-blower line and makes lurid accusations. You are subject to humiliating and invasive interviews, including the baseless rumour that you had sex in a meeting room named Appalachian Trail. One of you feels compelled to resign. Six months and no job later, your relationship flatlines.

OR

You start to develop feelings for a colleague. Luckily for you, they are reciprocated. You let your respective bosses know (or if one of you supervises the other, you tell the appropriate authority). Your company is a member of the twenty-first century and recognises that romances are bound to happen when humans work closely together. They have a coherent framework to deal with this. It may require one of you to change roles or at least responsibilities. You decide how you want to proceed.

Turnaround Story

The company you invested in, UpStart, wins several projects. They do a fantastic job, and your employer is so impressed that they recommend UpStart to a few other firms. You are delighted as your equity is gaining value. Unfortunately, on a large tender, with stricter disclosure requirements, UpStart has to submit details of its directors, financials, and ultimate beneficial ownership. There's your name. Soon you're the subject of an investigation at your office and facing termination for failing to disclose outside business interests.

OR

When UpStart tenders for bids with your employer, you come forward and disclose your investment. You explain you invested early (long before UpStart tendered) to support a relative and that your investment is passive (you are not involved in the management or strategy-setting). Your employer can decide whether to request you liquidate the investment (strict) or just preclude you from any dealings with UpStart. Your Code will probably have some text like, "We should avoid investments that could affect, or appear to influence, their decision-making on behalf of the organisation." The decision, therefore, becomes about how or if your decision-making could be influenced.

Only Show in Town

You know how this one goes; it's similar to *mate's rates* and *turnaround story*. The main difference is if your employer finds you were involved in hiring multiple connected suppliers, you start to look like a fraudulent kingpin. You either get fired or made the next president of Russia.

OR

If you disclose, as the friendly Kiwis did, you can at least be removed from any purchasing decisions and processes involving linked companies.

Bringing It All Together

I've avoided one large area of conflicts of interest – professional services firms (including lawyers, advisors, and accountants), ensuring they're not acting against existing clients' best interests. For example, if UpStart is suing DownStart, and you are the advisor to the former, you cannot (or should not) act for the latter. I won't spend much more time on this, as it's glaringly apparent (yet seemingly causes consternation in some of these firms). Many of you reading will herald from legal or advisory backgrounds and be fully aware of this topic.

Back to the more common conflicts – the best-case and worst-case scenarios are exaggerated in all the cases above, but they're not a million miles from accuracy. The only difference is the disclosure of material information. Lies (including withholding the truth) have a horrid habit of biting people on the butt. The final point I'd add, which we'll cover in greater detail in later discussions on competition, is an obvious one – make it clear to your people that they should avoid working with, for, or investing in organisations that may conflict with their employer.

I gave and will give more scenarios because the concept of conflicts of interest is straightforward (if in doubt, disclose). Still, the application can be complex (how to define or identify *doubt*). Give your people scenarios and the chance to practise and discuss these topics. There's no real shortcut to this topic; it's a human problem requiring constant adaptation as the way we work evolves.

Sharing Isn't Caring

Conflicts of interest overlap extensively with information security, data privacy, insider trading, bribery, and broader fraud schemes (kickbacks, etc.). I'll try and walk the narrow line between confusing you with things we'll discuss later and explaining how each can become (or be perceived as) a conflict. Again, let's use some real case studies:

1. You work for a large accounting firm. Your friend, a small business owner, also provides accounting support. Your clients are mega-multinationals, and your friend's customers are mom & pop businesses. So, when they ask you to share some templates, you oblige.

2. You work for a large construction firm. You subcontract to local tradespeople frequently. Your partner does search engine optimisation for small businesses and sole traders. They ask you to download the emails of the tradespeople for a mailing campaign. You agree as you still feel guilty about telling them what you *really* think of their parents.

3. You hear a rumour from a former colleague that a significant competitor is in financial difficulty. You tell your sister, who trades as a hobby. She shorts the competitor's stocks and buys you that watch you've been eyeing for ages.

4. You're still at the construction firm (yet to get busted for ripping out tradespeople's data). A friend's firm is bidding on a large contract. They ask you to reveal information about competitor tenders; in exchange, they'll get their firm to remodel the kitchen you always wanted.

5. Still not in jail, your friend bidding for the large contracts asks you to find out whether your analytics and audits focus on variable costs (cement, in particular). You think not, and your friend starts overcharging for cement, awarding you a share of the spoils in return.

I know, I know, *you* would never do any of these things. But those naughty *other* people do, repeatedly. Unfortunately, as risk professionals, we must always look at any system and think, "how could I break it?" If you consider times when you've made unwise decisions, how many of those have involved coercion or encouragement from people around you? Has someone in your family ever forced you to compromise your ethical standards?

We must accept that personal relationships will (and perhaps should) trump loyalty to organisations that will fire us if we stop achieving their goals. Organisations can range from ruthless to benevolent, but the threshold where they stop caring about you will usually be much lower than that of friends and family. The trick is to accept that conflicts of interest are not some dirty secret we must hide. I dislike the phrase conflicts of interest, as it inherently implies dissonance when often these issues are resolved with a simple disclosure.

A more straightforward way to phrase the issue is to ask people where their personal and professional lives might overlap. That is abstract, so we will need to provide some leading examples, which is why I chose the headings for this section: outside employment and side hustles; friends and family; and sharing (information) isn't caring. A former colleague, now working in-house in sub-Saharan Africa, often in rural communities where personal and work overlap, says she asks people to "unburden yourself and tell me where work meets personal life". I like the idea of unburdening yourself – secrets are heavy.

If you're after a slightly less esoteric and more prescriptive framework, how's this?:

1. Does it interfere with my responsibilities and my employer's expectations?

2. Am I using my employer's resources or my position for personal gain?

3. Could my (in)actions appear to be a conflict of interest to other people?

4. Do my actions compete with the interests of my employer?

If any of the above questions are *yes*, there is a potential conflict of interest.

Once again, linking back to values will help us. It would not be unreasonable to expect professional advisors bound by confidentiality to value discretion. Re-emphasising this value in your training and communication will help provide a principles-based construct to answer the four questions.

Endnote

1. "Family" includes your spouse or life partner, siblings, parents, in-laws, and children.

5
GIVING AND RECEIVING

Giving and receiving are usually treated as a subset of anti-bribery and anti-corruption (ABAC). But I think it's time we extended the concept beyond ABAC, where everyone trips up on different laws instead of the lucidity of a beginner's mindset. To explain what I mean, an American friend gave ABAC training to a group of Vietnamese entrepreneurs. He used the tried and tested definition: "giving cash or cash equivalents in return for an improper benefit". A bright spark in the audience asked, "There are approximately 11,500 lobbyists registered with your Congress. The price of basic medications in your country is typically 2.5 times more than comparable developed countries in Europe. How is that not giving cash or cash equivalents for improper benefit?"

I know some of you may think about regulation in lobbying or how it can be a force for positive change (e.g., shifting energy policy), but whenever you are giving or receiving, obsess less on the law and more on intention and appearance. Other areas I want to delve into include sponsorships and donations. All can be vehicles for positive change, just as much as car crashes of corruption. Similarly, conflicts of interest, which we just discussed and fraud (which we'll get to) frequently involve inappropriate or illegal giving and receiving of *stuff*.

By the end of this chapter, we should have put some meat on the bones of my favourite types of questions: why, who, what, when, and how. I don't usually start with *why*, as it's a difficult question to lead in any investigative or information-gathering context. However, it can save a monstrous amount of time here.

- Why are we considering giving or receiving anything?

- Who is giving and receiving?

- What is or will be offered/received?

- When is this happening?

- How is the transaction (and it is a transaction) occurring?

In many organisations, the legalistic (of value, for benefit) structure of the guidance, policy and approval framework becomes a semantic vortex of pointlessness. Compliance officers are subsumed in questions and cases regarding travel, conferences, coffee shops, and concerts, which are not a productive use of time and resources.

Some respond to this chaos with a stringent interpretation. For example, a major tech company has such strict policies that a friend (working in marketing) visited a Thai client, who gave them a bottle of sweet chilli sauce (worth less than $3), which they had to refuse politely.

Other organisations might prefer limits, for instance, ceilings for the amounts you can spend per person, per meal. These limits don't travel well. I remember working with a Finnish organisation entering Laos; their EUR 250 per head meal allowance might make sense in Helsinki but it provides a lot of leeway for funny business in Vientiane. You can vary the limits, in line with local costs of living. That might work. But it will require regular monitoring and updating as things change

Finally, some take a principles (or case-by-case) approach, which can be sensible if people understand, agree with, and respect the framework. If they don't, it's a total mess. The approach typically uses words like *reasonable, proportionate,* and *modest* to keep us on the straight and narrow. The challenge is that usually, one person's *reasonable* is another's *lavish.* I was working in the City of London very early in my career. A senior exec's phone rang, and a colleague picked it up. After muffled enquiry, he replied, "Oh, no, you won't catch him at his desk at this time; he'll be at lunch, at the oyster bar." It was 3.30 p.m. Spending hundreds of pounds a week on bubbly and slippery sea creatures was *reasonable* for that team.

Child's Play

Maybe a more direct parallel is parenting, precisely at that age when your child has some pocket money and access to confectionary (usually at or on the way to school). You can confiscate their pocket money and give them a packed lunch of delicious kale, hummus, quinoa, and all the things kids love. See how that works out for you in the long term. We weren't quite that strict in our daughter's case, but we did pack maybe one-too-many *healthy snacks* (a tautology). She is a budding cartoonist and started sketching scenes for friends and selling them, building up a secret sweetie slush fund augmented by petty larceny at home.

Next, you could go down the "acceptable limits" route. If your kid is feeling bold or annoyed with you, they'll look at the ceiling of the limit and go for broke – where can I derive maximum fun with the allocated budget? Again, not the behaviour we're trying to encourage.

Finally, you can take the principles approach, explaining healthy choices and blah. That strategy can work, but you must invest time explaining everything – the implications of decisions, how and when to treat yourself, things to avoid, etc. It might work if they understand, agree, and respect those principles (*proportionate, modest, reasonable,* etc.). After a few years with our daughter, we're getting there, but it's required a solid framework.

Now let's examine the challenges you might face and see if we can help you pick a framework that works for your organisation.

Beware Anyone (Including You) Bearing Gifts

Be afraid of gifts, hospitality, entertainment, travel, donations, sponsorships, the lot. Let's start with the basics. Why does an organisation need to give things to other people or entities? Years ago, I took to LinkedIn to crowdsource some of the best-worst ethical excuses my network had heard. We use many of these excuses to justify *why*, and I turned them into a bingo game (Figure 5.1).

Excuses that centre around "it's customary in the local culture" are often the hardest to shift. But shift, they will. If we look at the corruption crackdown in China – ignoring that it's primarily

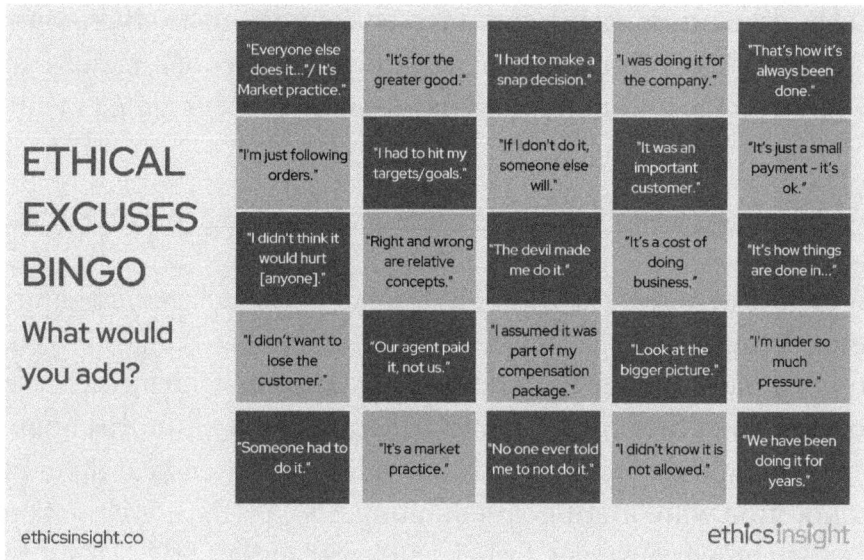

Figure 5.1 Ethical excuses bingo.

politically motivated to oust opposition and placate the urban elites who keep the Communist Party in power – it has moved the needle on the Lunar New Year gifting excesses. I'm not advocating a similar scorched-earth anti-corruption policy. I'm arguing that if a vast country with an ingrained culture of gifts-for-benefit has changed, the excuses above are bullshit.

I'm using *gifts* in this context very loosely as it's less of a mouthful than gifts, hospitality, entertainment, travel, donations, sponsorships, etc. I'm also avoiding *anything of benefit*, although it's a broader and probably better catch-all; more on that later. We could use the ethical excuses above with any of these categories:

- It's a market practice to sponsor healthcare professionals to attend our conferences.

135

- It was an important customer, so I agreed to fly them over (first class, with a weekend stay, on us) to our factory to inspect the multimillion-dollar equipment they wanted to buy (true story).

- It was just a small sponsorship to keep the local mayor sweet.

Some of the other excuses could broadly be bucketed as ignorance, being a sheep, it's for the greater good, I did it for you, and if I hadn't, something terrible would have happened. These excuses sit at the core of many challenges outlined in this book. But I brought the bingo in here because you'll often hear them in connection with offering or requesting ANYTHING. We'll get on to your brown envelope bribery and corruption. Still, I want to first linger on gifts (in the broadest sense).

So why start with gifts, not cash (bribes, kickbacks, grease payments, etc.)?

Why Gifts Trump Cash

One school of thought, which isn't unreasonable, suggests that gifts (and the rest) replace cash (transactive currencies) because they're easier to conceal. I don't think that's entirely it. Perhaps the gift might help disguise the benefit in some circumstances without drawing too much attention. For example, in real estate development deals in places with high levels of corruption, you will expect to see officials involved in granting land approvals living in the newly built condo they didn't pay for. To my mind, that is a gift (living rent-free or transferring ownership of a property) substituting cash in a less immediately obvious way.

In other cases, the gift has little to do with concealment. I remember seeing large military-grade European-made sports utility vehicles (SUVs) in Ho Chi Minh City, Vietnam. The absence of number plates prompted me to ask one of my contacts what was happening. They explained that former Soviet Union countries (who retain strong links from the USSR era) would bung Vietnamese officials anything sizeable and European to secure lucrative contracts. The pimped-up rides had become a symbol of corrupt opulence – no self-respecting kleptocratic apparatchik should leave home without one.

Vehicles that even Hollywood superstars might consider "a bit much" are hard to conceal; wire transfers into offshore bank accounts aren't.

There's a more fundamental psychological reason why gifts are so popular – they distance us from the act. Have you ever stolen stationery from work, a pen from a hotel, or sweets from the Woolworth's Pick 'n' Mix – a rite of passage in the UK for many of us 1980s kids? Would you have pilfered the cash equivalent of the stationery? Would you steal from petty cash or a store's cash register?

A body of research by Professor Dan Ariely discusses our sliding ethics when cash substitutes replace cash. Ariely's research is widely accessible in various books and the documentary *(Dis) Honesty: The Truth About Lies.*[1] Ariely conducted experiments where students self-scored a test they had taken in return for rewards. When his team substituted cash with tokens, we lied approximately twice as much about our scores, even if the counter where we exchanged the tickets for money was adjacent to the desk where we submitted our scores.

Gifts are – it would seem – easier to justify than wads of cash.

Why Ask Why?

Recognising this dissonance between accepting plain-old grubby cash and SUVs, *why* becomes a more powerful question than asking *what* the gift is. Asking why forces an examination of motive and allows us to follow up with more why questions. In Chapter 1, I gave the example of the Vietnamese healthcare company where sales reps had paid doctors handsomely to rent a room, allegedly to demonstrate a product. Let's now put that scenario through the *why* test.

1. Why are we considering paying thousands of dollars to rent a room for a short period?

   Ans: Because the HCPs said if we wanted to demo our products, we needed to pay a rental fee to use a theatre in the hospital.

2. Why did the HCPs not make this request previously?

3. Why is the rental fee so high?

4. Why do we need a theatre to demo the products when we didn't before?

5. Why did you agree?

These questions may seem hostile and harsh, but you see how they're very hard to answer without exposing the true intention of the gift. If you want a more benign strategy to approve or deny gift requests, this test might help:

- Convince me it's legal, moral, and safe.

This statement came from my good friend, Pat Poitevin, who spent 25 years in the Royal Canadian Mounted Police as an investigator. Pat used this strategy with his three daughters during their teen years. Any framework that can withstand teenagers will generally work in an organisational environment.

Play around with the statement, linking to what you're about as an organisation. The trick is to put the onus on the person giving (or requesting approval to offer) the *gift* to justify why it's a good idea and poses no ethical problems. If they cannot meet that fairly basic threshold, you don't need to ask the other questions.

The Other Questions

Now, let's assume the gift has passed the *why* test – the subsequent questions are a bit more straightforward. I'd use *why* questions here, too; *why* the local mayor, a new Rolex, *and why now*?

- **Who:** Alarm bells should ring for anyone with whom you're negotiating, wooing, disagreeing, or appeasing. Sub-questions should consider:

  - If there are too many people involved or invited.

  - If it is unclear why certain people are involved (for example, partners and spouses of clients).

- Anything involving public officials (aside from the apparent corruption risk, you may also be required to record any gifts under local legislation).

- **What:** Beware anything expensive, inappropriate, or controversial.

- **When:** The rule is quite simple here – don't give anything too often or when negotiating. Some folks will try and get around per meal (or equivalent) limits by taking people out frequently. If you're negotiating, giving someone something seldom looks like anything other than an attempt to influence their decision.

- **How:** Any opacity should be a concern. For instance, you later find donations to an unknown charity are linked to a minister approving your license.

If I now expand on what my catch-all use of gifts might include and how and why people use these inducements, you will hopefully see how useful simple question frameworks become. Your aim – in most organisations – is not to kill all giving and receiving; it is to implement a clinical triage tool that sifts out the problematic requests.

If you're curious how I'd condense all of this down, Figure 5.2 is an attempt to do just that.

Anything of Value

My son loves vehicles; I'm less enamoured. If I offered him tickets to the F1, I could probably extort a Victorian workload

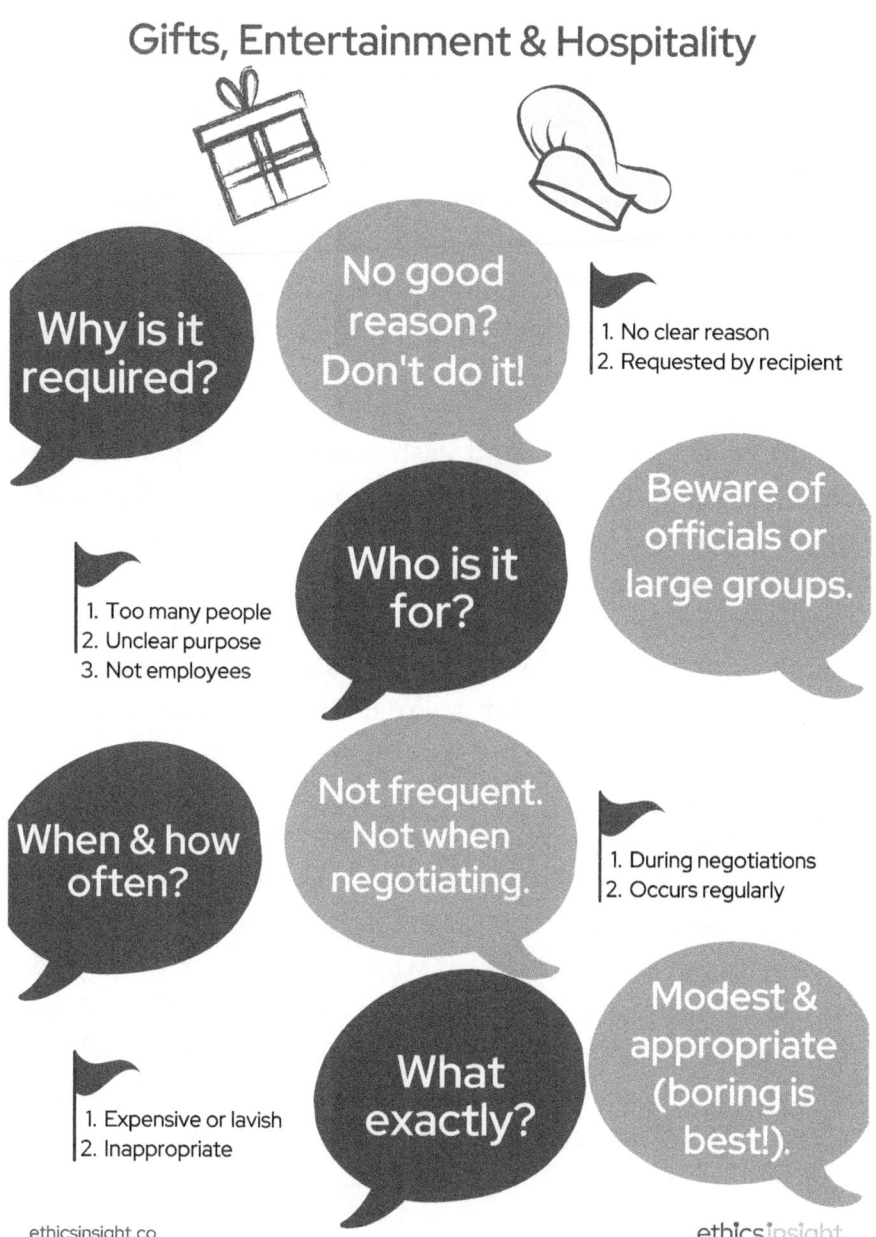

Figure 5.2   Gifts, entertainment and hospitality: dealing with confusion.

of chores. If we tried that same negotiation with me, we'd get nowhere. *Value* is intensely personal. Some things will generally have value for most people. We must create a hierarchy in a clear framework for approving or rejecting anything of value. At the top, we put those things that generally have a currency (pun intended) for most people. The aim is to create a simple filtration system to sift out the more ethically questionable requests, allowing us time to focus where your expertise is needed (things of relative value).

At the top, we have cash and cash equivalents – gold, shares, jewellery, watches, property, land, non-fungible tokens, etc. Anything you can (relatively easily) transact in open markets. It's tough – in almost all cases – to justify giving or receiving anything in this bracket. Corporate-branded notepads and pens generally don't have immense resale value, so these items are usually acceptable (assuming you're not plastering your logo on luxury pens or alike).

The next layer consists of consumables – meals, holidays, tickets, entertainment, hospitality, conferences, etc. These items are more experiential and less transferable. Given those constraints, our *why* questions can focus on why them, why now, why that particular consumable? Our triage filter should also sift out anything controversial (hunting, strip clubs, alcohol-centric chaos). As a former FBI prosecutor once said to an audience of business leaders, "If you'd rather not attend, it's probably okay. If it's fun, forget it."

The final step is the murkiest and most challenging. We need to create frameworks that efficiently triage the previous two layers to allow us time to focus on favours – jobs (usually for relatives), access (e.g., you sit on a college admission board), sex, skullduggery, etc. I know of a particularly seedy private investigator who transported doctored semen for a married client facing a paternity claim across the Malaysian border with Singapore. In exchange, the PI received ongoing contracts from the multinational firm the child abandoner headed. Most of your colleagues will know that this level of *value* is dodgy, but it bears repeating and emphasis in training. There have been many scandals involving sex for contracts (even in Singapore's supposedly squeaky-clean defence sector) and jobs for feckless relatives in return for ongoing work (Western banks in China, for instance).

Sponsorships and Donations

As the net has tightened in the world of gifts, corrupt-minded shysters have doubled down on sponsorships and donations. That is not to say philanthropic, community, or social impact projects are dirty. You should be careful when you're approached to donate or sponsor something. Given the cases I've worked on, I could spend an age on this section where spurious non-governmental organisations (NGOs) or charities have extorted cash and later channelled it to corrupt politicians, insurgents, terrorists, or organised criminals.

A rattled port operator called a few years back. An NGO had been widely quoted in local newspapers alleging worker mistreatment and other violations. No one had heard of this NGO. Our intelligence gathering revealed the NGO was linked to the port authority, who had repeatedly tried to extract cash bribes (to renew the licence without undue interference). When the operator refused, they put their best man on the job. The port authority owned a major food market in a tourist haven. They had an enforcer who would extract ever-steeper rent from stallholders with any necessary coercion, including beatings and scolding using red-hot kitchen implements. This lovely chap had a second job – running a newly formed NGO that bribed journalists to publish assassination pieces for anyone resisting his masters' bribes.

This tale is not an outlier. My message is, therefore, straightforward, go through every request for sponsorship and donations with a fine toothcomb to try and establish:

1. The charity or community group is legitimate and appropriately registered (charities and NGOs must register in many countries).

2. You know the identity of the individual(s) behind the entity in question.

3. You are not donating to the charity or community at the request of an official or businessperson with whom you have ongoing or potential dealings.

4. That the recipient of the funds will disperse them appropriately – this can require oversight (including audit rights) to ensure that funds are not misused.

Ideally, seize the initiative by being proactive about your community and social engagement plan. It becomes easier to sift out illegitimate requests if you define how you intend to contribute, with whom, and the terms.

Why Do Organisations Play These Games?

I've alluded to many reasons folks fall foul of the scams and scandals outlined above. But it bears a brief refresher. We make these mistakes to win, avoid, or gain.

- **Win:** secure contracts, rig bids, fix prices, secure kickbacks, and all that bad stuff.

- **Avoid:** fines, sanctions, overlooking (tax, licences, requirements, violations), etc.

- **Gain:** expedited approvals, competitive information, access, prestige, etc.

These examples are not exhaustive, but I include them as there can be a tendency to assume that people give things to get good things in return. It is often more complex than that. Our old friend, the *why* question helps us here, but so do solid training and communication. We need to get colleagues thinking about the potential risks of giving or receiving three-dimensionally – considering what is value, understanding who is ultimately involved, and recognising that the *benefit* can also include avoiding harm.

Bringing It All Together

The previous sections may seem a bit of a mood-killer, but there is still plenty of room to entertain, support, and charm your stakeholders. The trick is quite simple – focus on the overall benefit to a community of stakeholders, not transacting value with specific individuals in decision-making positions.

Once again, go back to who you intend to be in the world. Where on the spectrum do you sit – Wolf of Wall St or refusing $3 bottles of sweet chilli sauce? The complexity and explanations I've given highlight many pitfalls, but the solutions are simple – *why* are we considering this? Run the subsequent *why* questions through a filter centred on your values (what you deem reasonable and acceptable) to triage the issues requiring examination to a bare minimum.

The policy, training, or communication you develop should include brief examples relevant to your operational realities (defined in the risk assessment we discussed earlier).

Endnote

1. https://www.imdb.com/title/tt2630898/

6
ETHICAL TRANSACTIONS

In the previous chapters, we dealt with issues with broad applicability. Values, expectations, responding to problems, and treating others with respect are – I would imagine – constructs all organisations must consider. I've also yet to meet an organisation where personal and professional lives don't occasionally conflict and giving or receiving happens in most cultures and contexts.

Now it's time to get into the weeds of ethics, compliance, business integrity, whatever you call it. I will cover a lot of ground – including anti-bribery and anti-corruption, fair competition, insider trading, trade sanctions, anti-money laundering, due diligence, and monitoring. The last two topics should be relevant for any organisation heading into the M territory of SME (small and medium enterprises) or beyond. Finding a catch-all for that broad list of issues is challenging, but I'll go with ethical transactions. We won't cover every area in sufficient detail for you to walk away with a concrete plan. This is a book, not a manual. But I will try and highlight the main pain points I've observed and offer tips and guidance on how to address them.

Some of these areas are subject to stringently enforced national and international laws and regulations, which often overlap. I will not be providing you with gonzo legal analysis or advice. My role focuses on the application (enforcement) of these laws, as I've investigated and assisted more than 25 organisations responding to possible or actual regulatory actions.

Some may be wondering about the difference between international and national laws. Much legislation – mainly from the US or (current and former) European Union countries – has transnational applications. Without getting into the technicalities too much, the key term is "extraterritorial", allowing the prosecutor to pursue cases beyond their geographic borders. The best example is the US Foreign Corrupt Practices Act (FCPA). The Department of Justice uses the FCPA to prosecute people and companies internationally. The legislation establishes *jurisdiction* (the licence to prosecute) through various means, including anyone with a US incorporated presence, US nationals as employees, transactions with US entities, etc. If you type "FCPA fines" into your search engine of choice, you'll see that many non-US firms and people have been prosecuted and pursued (successfully) for wrongdoings beyond US borders.

If you feel this Team America World Police approach is heavy-handed or unfair – like the Vietnamese entrepreneur in Chapter 5 discussing lobbying – that's too bad. The US prosecutorial system is not going anywhere, and other countries follow suit. The US model typically sees prosecuting agencies retaining (a significant portion of) the fines they dole out, which they then use to boost capacity and resources.

This extraterritorial reach has not created a level playing field yet. Firms that steer clear of US (or European) jurisdiction continue to fly under the radar. I've lost count of the gripes from leaders and salespeople bemoaning how "[*Other* nationality] firms can still do all this funny business." But many internationalised organisations have (or aspire to have) operations in or connected to US and European markets.

Furthermore, I'm not aware of any countries that have legalised corruption, money laundering, or other integrity crimes. Even if the domestic enforcement is weak – as it is in most places, including many developed markets – it may not remain so. Not breaking the law is generally a good idea!

The standards I will focus on are best practice (i.e., high threshold) legislation. Most of the time, these guidelines come from the US, but not always. The reasons I don't want to get into the exact reach of each piece of legislation are:

1. Dear reader, I don't know where you are!

2. It would send you to sleep.

3. You need to get legal advice if you're concerned about which laws and regulations might impact you.

4. In the past 20 years, I've seen more convergence than divergence – wherever you operate, regulations are generally static or trending up.

If your organisation takes a pure compliance approach to regulation – if it's technically legal, it's okay – I think you may be on the wrong side of history. The organisations I work with look at the universe of regulation and pick the highest benchmark. Aside from the potential ethical upsides, this is a very sensible strategy for other reasons, including:

- It's easier for people to follow – having different rules across global organisations is a recipe for confusion and disaster.

- It's easier to develop consistent content (training, policies, guides, etc.) – reducing workload.[1]

- It reduces the need to monitor a vast spectrum of laws in intricate detail – as regulation (usually) moves quite slowly.[2]

If you feel specific topics are irrelevant to you – or better still, your risk assessment helped you focus – that makes total sense. I will go through each issue individually so you can dip in and out of this chapter.

I'll start with anti-bribery and anti-corruption for two reasons. The considerations and structures you'd need to manage this risk are relevant to the following areas. As mentioned in the Introduction, corruption is the grease that oils almost all ills covered in this book. It is the endgame Boss Baddy. If human trafficking, environmental degradation, illegal wildlife trading, paedophilia, and everything else revolting offends you, this is the area to focus your efforts. Corruption is the currency of evil.

Anti-Bribery and Anti-Corruption

Chapters 4 and 5 – giving and receiving and conflicts of interest – overlap considerably with anti-bribery and anti-corruption (ABAC).

Most enforcement agencies consider it illegal to gift an official an expensive watch or hire their useless nephew to secure favourable tender specifications on a government contract. In these cases, the timepiece and employment would be considered a *benefit*, which led to your receiving an *unfair advantage* (the favourable tender specifications).

Therefore, I'll focus less on the mechanics of benefit – giving, receiving, conflicts of interest, and money – and more on ABAC challenges and what to do about them. But first, it's worth re-emphasising that cash bribes extend well beyond brown envelopes – encompassing currencies (traditional and crypto), precious metals, shares, jewellery, property, land, and non-fungible tokens.

Your ABAC framework should consider what, how and who. What could be used to corrupt? How that would work – would you transact directly and openly or indirectly, hoping to conceal the deal? Who would it involve (giving and receiving)? Most ABAC training follows that approach. It makes sense, as you want people to think broadly about value (given how subjective and relative it can be). Then you need to explain that bribes don't need to be made directly to get you in trouble; the legal wording is usually something like *acts committed on your behalf*. Finally, there's often a cursory examination of generic *officials* and maybe reference to "private to private bribery". At this point, most people are asleep. If you want to summarise the topic, do so, as in Figure 6.1; don't make it half of your training.

I like to work backwards, as it's a simpler and smaller dataset. But before getting to who, how, and what, let's briefly define bribery and corruption. Bribery is giving someone something to influence

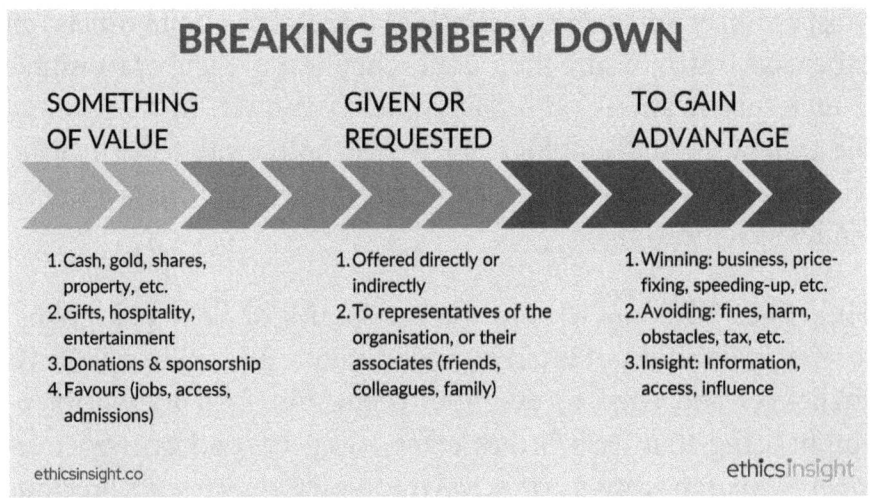

Figure 6.1   Breaking bribery down.

their actions (ideally in your favour). Corruption is when bribes lead to officials doing things they should not (to your benefit). We should define officials very broadly, covering any government employee (including police and military) and extending to employees of entities the government wholly or majority owns (e.g., utility providers, transport companies, etc.).

Why is it necessary to distinguish officials? Because the FCPA and many local laws will usually define corruption in the context of public officials. Other legislation, including the UK Bribery Act, extends to private bribery, ostensibly business-to-business. I'd always suggest picking the higher threshold because it's less confusing. It's weird to tell your folks they can't bribe officials, but bribing private clients should be considered case-by-case, depending on relevant local laws. Not exactly a compelling message and testament to your standards of integrity.

Now let's ask your colleagues, "Who is a real pain in the ass to deal with?"

Who's a Pain in the Ass?

I appreciate that asking this question could provide an expansive list in many organisations. Let's add a preface to make it easier, hopefully. "Who won't do what they're meant to without special treatment or extra incentives?" If that's too much of a mouthful, ask frontline teams, "Who do you deal with outside the organisation?" You explain you don't need to know every single person. We can start with broad categories and drill down if we need to. The Department of Agriculture is enough detail – if distinctions between fisheries, aquaculture, or land management are required, that'll become evident.

Write those entities in a column on a whiteboard (or virtual equivalent), aggregating them into groups. For example, my business looks like this:

1. Corporate registry – government

2. Tax authorities – government

3. Financial services companies – banks, wire transfer systems, etc.

4. Lawyers and advisors (accountants, etc.)

5. Advisors – marketing, website, platform, recruiters, etc.

6. Vendors – subscriptions, IT products, freelancers, etc.

7. Partners – other advisors, strategic alliances, etc.

8. Landlord

9. Utility providers

10. Clients

11. Competitors

12. Professional associations

13. Conference organisers, journalists, publications

When brought up to this level, the longest list I've seen (so far) was 70 entities for a huge multinational. It should be around 20–30 groups for most of you and shouldn't take too long. You'll see I've lumped some quite bulky groups together, intentionally. Their benefit to us (me) is similar. Lawyers and accountants provide assurance, advice, and compliance with various requirements. Conference organisers, journalists, and multiple publications might ask us for content (or an appearance). In return, we get a platform. The benefit is the key here – as I've mentioned before, in ABAC, we're concerned with getting things you shouldn't.

It's easier to answer the following question with entities grouped by what they offer us. "Could any of these entities make extra requests to give us special treatment?" Or, more pointedly, "If we gave any of these entities extra benefits, would it help us?" If you cast your mind back to Chapter 5, I explained how benefit is not just a vehicle to win things (new deals, renewal business, etc.). It's also to avoid harm or gain information, preferential treatment, or access. You will need to emphasise this point repeatedly.

I appreciate it takes trust to get people to answer these questions honestly, so I like to use anonymous (and ideally fun and interactive) voting tools. You can ask people to vote on scales (unlikely to likely) if those scales are simple and intuitive to use. Three buttons (yes, no, maybe) will also help if that won't work. Armed with a traffic light system to roughly estimate who of your stakeholder universe might be corruptible, we have triaged down the dataset. Sometimes this will involve a bit of sub-categorisation, for example, only two entities have tried to extract bribes from me: freelancer vendors and publications. I'd therefore need to pull them out and not tar other vendors, conference organisers, and journalists with the same brush.

I appreciate I run a small advisory business registered in low corruption risk markets (Singapore and the UK) – focused on ethics (!) – so I am not a good overall indicator of ABAC risk. However, thornier assessments I've run (including energy in Myanmar, Brazilian healthcare, defence sector in North Africa, and forestry in Russia) seldom return a complete sea of red (using the traffic lights risk system).

How Might We Be Devious?

Armed with a list of potentially problematic stakeholders, let's consider how we could corrupt them. Would you turn up at their office with an envelope (suitcase) of cash? Probably not. You may need to prime people a little here with examples, including:

1. Using intermediaries to facilitate the transaction.
2. Using offshore accounts and structures.

3. Concealing the payments in existing financial mechanisms (e.g., rebates).

4. Purchasing products or services from entities connected to the person(s) you're trying to bribe.

5. Channelling the bribes through family members of the corrupt person(s).

The majority of FCPA cases involve intermediaries. I've worked in more than 50 (mainly emerging market) countries, and in each, very few people are naive to the chosen payment method. In the former Soviet Union countries, for the first two decades of the 2000s, Cypriot special purpose vehicles (companies set up for a transaction) were ubiquitous in dirtbag deals. We're creatures of habit, lemmings, to be precise. The chosen routes for corrupt payments will vary from place to place (not as much as some country analysts claim), and your local colleagues will know the rules of the game.

For some of your colleagues, it may seem unfair that you can be prosecuted for the actions of a third-party (partner, agent, intermediary, supplier, etc.). We (and regulators) are concerned about what they do on your behalf. It's no longer sufficient to say, "I had no idea that the $25 million management fee my agent requested would be used to bribe the oil minister." If we're asking people to represent us and our interests, we must explain and enforce our expected standards of integrity. In some cases, you will need to emphasise this point with examples of how third parties might corrupt others to your benefit.

You should now have a triaged dataset of red (and amber) potentially dodgy stakeholders and a list of usually around five (maximum ten) ways these transactions would typically go down.

Now, reverse the exercise, and ask how people might influence us (suppliers, vendors, and advisors). Bribery is a game of give *and* take.

What Do Corruptible Types Like?

Now we can get to the benefits part. Thinking of all possible items of value – which we've already established can be highly subjective – is a very abstract way to introduce a concept. With some names to work with, it should be easier. Ask your colleagues how the potential miscreants might like to receive their ill-gotten benefit.

Another reason to ask this question last: it changes with the times. For example, in 2010–2011, when the Vietnamese currency (the Dong) was devalued repeatedly, corrupt politicians chose to receive their bungs in gold bullion. This preference, coupled with ordinary Vietnamese offshoring wealth, made Vietnam a key gold trading partner with Switzerland for a few months. Some estimates suggested that up to 40% of the nation's wealth was gold. With a booming economy, officials had moved on to the military-grade SUVs four years later. At the time of writing, the only constant scheme (in Vietnam) throughout this period has been officials awarding deals contingent on your organisation using a designated list of suppliers. These vendors usually include a blend of legitimate enterprises owned by people the official wants to keep happy (other officials, family members, prominent supporters, etc.) and some absolute turkeys (useless shell companies created to transact kickbacks).

You should know how bribery and corruption might manifest in your organisation – who, how, and what. I am not suggesting your policies and training only extend to these people and areas. I suggest you avoid what I see in most policies and training – a broad-brush and blanket approach to ABAC, covering every possible angle and sending most of your audience away confused or rested (after a good nap). Introduce the topic broadly – giving or receiving anything of value to influence someone's actions, directly or indirectly. My 11-year-old understands bribery as a concept, and most of your colleagues will. What needs highlighting and later addressing with proper training, communication, and controls is how bribery could impact your operations: who, how, what.

Giving to Get Something You Should Receive

Before we move on, a subset of ABAC causes consternation and confusion. What if we pay an official to make them do their job correctly? The UK Bribery Act calls this a facilitation payment and explicitly prohibits such payments. The US FCPA asks you to record (in your *Books & Records*) all such payments. In much of the world, simple bureaucratic steps – like getting licences approved, goods through customs on time (and undamaged), or immigration permits – come with requests for facilitation payments. Organisations with the dreaded *zero tolerance* for facilitation payments are huge or deluded. Mega-corps have leverage most can only dream of. They can call up someone senior in the local government to squash the pesky official making the demand.

A few years back, I was involved in a study that asked senior leaders in European and US headquarters of multinationals if they felt facilitation payments were an issue for their organisation. Approximately 25% thought they might be. We'd also asked the frontline employees of these organisations in complex emerging markets the same question, and their response suggested a figure over 70%.

I'd agree with that assessment, having worked in the former (frontline) most of my career. It's probably even higher as our dataset focused mainly on large multinationals with significant leverage. Therefore, if you're honest (and operating internationally), I'd suggest following a policy of working towards the elimination of facilitation payments. In the final chapter, we'll look at some resistance strategies to help you become a more challenging target for extortive requests. Figure 6.2 provides a simple way to identify facilitation payments.

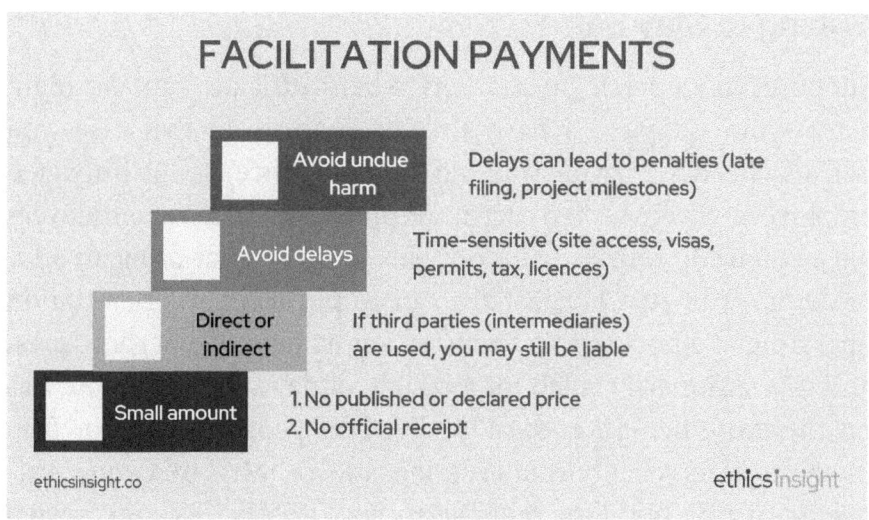

Figure 6.2   Facilitation payments explained.

As for the million-dollar question (or often multimillion dollar fine), should you record the payments and risk violating the UK (and other legislation) to comply with the FCPA? Yes. Why? Because not recording makes you look like you're concealing, which you are. It's generally better to demonstrate that you're trying to right wrongs rather than hiding them.

The UK Act also includes a provision that states you need to demonstrate you did everything you could to prevent bribery. Failure to show adequate procedures and controls sets a high benchmark. But suggestions it's a significant shift in approach are misguided. The US legislation and often local enforcement will and does make a judgement about the appropriateness of your framework. This assessment will inform the aggression of prosecution and the severity of penalties – all the more reason to demonstrate and document your efforts to establish an appropriate framework.

Bribing to Stay Safe

Suppose you operate in markets where officials can or might extort your people. Or have already done so. In that case, you will also need to provide training (and guidance) to any impacted employees. I've worked on multiple issues where employees have received requests from officials with a threat of harm and/ or denial of liberty. For instance, an employee of an organisation operating at a port in India refused a port master's illegal request and was summarily jailed for a couple of days. That example was on the more benign end, sadly. I've had people break down in interviews, relaying border crossings at the barrel of a gun, beatings with rifle butts for refusing to pay "access fees", and sexual harassment or rape (euphemistically called sextortion), usually at the hands of the local law enforcement. No organisation is worth sacrificing your safety and liberty for. Have the courtesy to tell your people as much. If they fear for their safety or freedom, pay the bribe, notify your superiors as soon as it's safe, and record full details of the payment.

Yes, we have different thresholds, and some people will pay too soon and too much, as they get spooked by vague threats, whereas others will stand firm and sometimes have officials back down. You can finesse your guidance as you better calibrate the seriousness of the threat posed by different stakeholders. But as a benchmark, aim low. You don't want your folks feeling they have to risk life and limb for what is usually a few dollars (local equivalent) – think back to your values. Who do you want to be as an organisation?

Fair Dealings and Competition

What a wishy-washy title. Fair dealings? Competition – is that a good thing (or a bad thing)? I agree. It's a confusing topic, made worse by other jargon, like anti-trust, anti-competitive practices, and unfair competition. Maybe this is easier: don't act like a gang. The laws here are trying to stop you from ganging up with (some of) your competitors to distort the market. How might that manifest in real life? Here are a few (not exhaustive) examples:

- **Price-fixing:** Collusion to set prices.

- **Reseller price maintenance:** Resellers are not allowed to set independent prices.

- **Exclusive dealing:** Mandating that third party only purchases from one supplier.

- **Dividing regions:** An agreement by competitors to refrain from operating in agreed-upon territories.

- **Limit-pricing:** The price discourages others from entering the market.

- **Dumping:** Selling at a loss to drive out the competition before rising prices later.

- **Discriminatory doctrines:** Restricting certain activities and/ or sectors to particular groups (often religious or ethnic).

Hopefully, you get the general idea. I will not spend an age going through how unfair practices might occur. If you're big enough an organisation for this to be an issue, you can afford professional advice! Your advisors will also be able to explain how unfair competition laws differ worldwide, often to reflect local market peculiarities. For example, in Korea, chaebols (large industrial conglomerates) are so prominent that unfair competition is a daily dilemma. In Malaysia, local laws that favour ethnic Malay Muslims preclude other groups from key strategic sectors – a discriminatory law.

Rather than get caught in these weeds, let's focus on common pain points and how to avoid them.

Get Out Your Crystal Ball

Fair competition is one of the most dynamic areas of risk. The state of flux partly reflects market conditions – as new sectors rise and older ones consolidate. Unfair competition is generally unpopular (particularly with impacted consumers). Politicians will often decry monopolistic (or oligopolistic) behaviours.

Let's use a scenario. A new government, Reformars, sweeps into power on an anti-corruption and anti-big-business platform. To spur the knowledge economy and help a young population compete require vastly improved telecommunications infrastructure. Reformars' leaders run a tender for a 5G network. Their advisors suggest choosing one winning bidder (rather than multiple companies implementing different technology and standards). A few years later, the winning bidder, Terrific Telco, has done a great job.

Sadly for Reformars (and their constituents), they've seriously mismanaged the economy and become as corrupt as their predecessors. After a routing in a general election, the victorious party, Liberatores, sweep to power on a good governance platform amidst soaring living costs. Liberatores highlight Terrific Telco as an example of Reformars' crony politics, noting their total monopoly on servicing and maintaining the 5G network. Liberatores blame the costs of telecommunications bills on Terrific Telco, ignoring the local network operators (who switched parties to back them). Local competition laws are vague and open to interpretation from a notoriously creaky, unqualified, and impressionable judiciary. Terrific Telco's assets are confiscated within a few months, and maintenance contracts are parsed out to firms connected to Liberatores.

This not-so theoretical example may seem on the extreme end of the spectrum, but watering down the scenario a tiny bit will bring in many regular allegations of price-fixing, bid-rigging, cartel behaviour, and distortive market practices levelled at slightly befuddled organisations. Businesses that don't consider perspective generally act surprised when some people don't like their dominance. They needed a crystal ball, or better still, some sensible scenario-planning.

Step Back and Analyse

If your organisation is highly successful and increasing its market share, that may seem great, but it comes with associated risks. Similarly, if you're in a period of consolidation – mergers and acquisitions – that may herald stability, but it also brings challenges. Finally, if you're the cooperative type, coming together with competitors to give clients the benefits of your collective genius, not everyone will be pleased.

Assess whether any of those conditions sound familiar and if they are, proceed cautiously. If you need a framework, it will need to be bespoke to your activities and operations, but a rough outline might do:

1. **Assess** your competitors and third-party landscape (if your business is contingent or heavily reliant on organisations with questionable competition credentials, be careful).

2. **Know the local laws:** if you operate in places where the law is open to interpretation by whoever controls the judiciary and regulators, skip this step and spend more time on step 4.

3. **Focus on any higher-risk areas** of your operations (e.g., if you're required to have a local partner in certain markets); consider where you might share sensitive information in your activities.

4. **Learn about the local enforcers' focus** as it may be very different to what's on paper – you may need to invest in government relations support. In this phase, you may have to factor in populist politics, geopolitical disputes, and anti-foreigner sentiment.

5. Having identified any potentially high-risk areas, **establish boundaries** between teams and partners.

6. **Train your people** on what to do if they hear or see information they probably shouldn't, and help them understand what not to say.

Point 5 can be very challenging for organisations that regularly cooperate with others. For example, I worked with a construction engineering firm that routinely joined consortiums to realise large infrastructure projects. Their people will be working side-by-side with competitors, sometimes for years, on these tasks. Friendships naturally form, and the lines between different organisations blur. In such situations, there are some controls – including segregation of duties and data and job rotations – but your best hope is to train people well.

Think of anti-competition training as a happy problem – you got so big and successful that you need it!

Insider Trading

You may wish to skim or skip this section if you're not working for, with, or closely linked to publicly traded companies. But it does include a case study about a hiker called Derek and vague references to (love) triangles.

Anti-competition's life partner is insider trading – but anti-comp doesn't know insider trading has been having an affair for years with conflicts of interest. This tawdry love triangle would make for a terrible graphic – I tried, a Venn diagram didn't work either. So let me explain instead. Insider trading involves the unauthorised disclosure of any non-public information. If you're wondering what that means in plain English, it's telling people secrets. If you work closely with competitors or friends and family (conflicts of interest), the chances of secrets slipping are much higher; hence the overlap between these three areas.

You've just shared secrets at this point, but insider trading occurs when you use these secrets to make investment trades and decisions. Let's use a simple example, Derek works in HR at EnormoCo, a large conglomerate. He's asked to join a secret project – vetting candidates to be the company's next CEO as the board has lost confidence in the incumbent as financial forecasts for Q4 are dire. Derek's hiking buddy, Deidre, is a part-time trader. They discuss why Derek has been so busy recently on a long trek over a weekend. Derek tells Deidre about the top-secret project at EnormoCo, asking Deidre to promise she won't tell anyone. Deidre doesn't tell anyone. Deidre trades EnormoCo's stock and makes a killing.

You may be thinking, how the hell would anyone know? In this case, you may well be right. If Deidre is a small-time trader, she may fly under the radar. But, sometimes, the Deidre figure might be an institutional investor, or there might be multiple Dereks leaking information. What information are we talking about? The operative term is *material* – any information that could be valuable to someone outside the business making investment decisions. When you unpack the list, it's pretty long. A few examples would include:

1. **Financial or market data:** results, projections, earnings, losses, dividends, distributions, policy changes, share splits, new equity or debt financing.

2. **Competitive environment:** mergers, joint ventures, acquisitions, consolidations, or any coming together (proposed, considered, or actual).

3. **Changes:** (possible) pricing changes, new products and developments, new technology, market entry, disposal or continuation of assets, subsidiaries, or activities, changes in leadership.

4. **Business deals:** big wins or losses, consortiums, ending contracts, renewals.

5. **Problems:** bankruptcy, cash flow or liquidity problems, work stoppages or production challenges, (threatened) litigation, regulatory actions, disputes.

It doesn't matter if the developments are positive or negative. If they (could) have value to someone, they're material.

The other operative phrase is "non-public" – something not previously disclosed or not otherwise available to the public. A more straightforward way to think of it: if it's not on the first few pages of Google, be careful. For example, your organisation, Leafium, is bringing out a new game-changing electric car battery. You type in "battery + Leafium", and the results show only existing products. Keep it to yourself. You can flip this the other way – if access to information requires a password, keycard, or meeting invite, keep it confidential.

Insider trading can occur when you use this material non-public information to trade, disclose it, or recommend someone else makes the trade (the conflicts of interest link).

The best way to socialise this concept with colleagues is to use an inverted pyramid (see, I managed to squeeze a triangle reference in again). At the top, where it's widest, you can use quickfire quizzes and situations to help people recognise what a broad bucket *material* covers. Use examples tailored to the user as you progress. For instance, with Derek, EnormoCo might have used scenarios and case studies about changes in leadership or integration of new employees following a proposed merger. Before lasering in on function-specific content, we need to open people's eyes to the bewildering amount of information they might freely disclose, which could get them into trouble.

Trade Controls and Sanctions

Global events frequently bring this topic into focus – from Russia's invasions, Iranian nuclear ambitions, Myanmar's coups, and North Korea's bellicose threats. For many of us, it can seem, at first glance, quite removed from our reality; it isn't. Outsourcing, decentralised supply chains, internationalisation of business, and increasingly global consumer demands create exposure. The shirt you're wearing might be a sanctions case study. Where were the constituent parts sourced, processed, and manufactured? Cotton from Xinjiang, coal (used to dye) from Zimbabwe, petroleum products from Venezuela, garment manufacture in Myanmar?

All these places have been (or are) subject to trade controls and sanctions.

It gets even more complex when we factor in re-routing, international shipping, wire transfers of money, and grey market activities. I've worked on many of these cases, and two always float to the top of my memory.

Pachinko parlours are very popular in Japan – brightly-lit rooms full of what look like slot machines (they're a bit more than that, but that's a tangent). Japanese residents of Korean ancestry run many of the companies controlling the venues. Some of them retain familial links to North Korea. A blend of coercion, threats, filial duty, organised criminal and historic ties ensures a flow of funds back to the impoverished dictatorship. But Japan (and many other countries) block all trade with Asia's primo pariah state. Luckily for the Kim dynasty, Cambodia (and others) remain on friendly terms. Cambodia has more licensed banks than a country of 20–25 million people mostly living below the poverty line should. It's also one of the most dollarised countries globally, a perfect place to set up a *no-questions-asked* bank. Converting pachinko yen into dollars in a Cambodian bank you own before moving some of those funds to North Korea is surprisingly easy. It's also flouting sanctions and money-laundering laws (more on the latter soon).

In the second case, a Japanese manufacturer of high-end drones noticed a significant spike in missing and shipped products from a Malaysian manufacturing facility. Malaysia is a hub of parallel trade and grey market practices. The country also retains low-key relations with North Korea (remember the assassination of Kim Jong-un's brother in Kuala Lumpur International airport?). You guessed it. The drones were shipped to North Korea (via China) to obfuscate their origin and destination. In North Korea, the drones were weaponised or used in reconnaissance operations. In the hierarchy of sanctions violations, sending weapons (or components) to lunatic despots is generally the biggest no-no.

Sanctions are complex, given the many moving parts. You need to know where you're sourcing from and where your products (and services) might end up. Before that, we should unpack what's involved and who enforces them.

What Is a Sanction?

Sanctions are penalties imposed by one nation (or a group of nations) on one (or more) other nations. They can be unilateral (imposed by one country) or multilateral (imposed by more countries). There are many distinctions within sanctions, but we should deal with the big ones first:

1. **Embargoes:** A ban on trade or commercial activity with a particular country (sector within a country), person, entity, or region. For example, broad country-level sanctions or those prohibiting defence (weapons) sales to a particular country.

2. **Quotas:** Trade restrictions imposed by a government limit the number (or value) of goods you can import during a particular period.

3. **Tariffs:** High(er) import or export taxes imposed by a government (usually to protect domestic producers).

4. **Asset freezes:** Preventing assets owned by sanctioned individuals and organisations from being moved or sold.

For example, preventing a dictator (and family members) from accessing and withdrawing money from overseas bank accounts.

Most of us, especially SMEs, don't have much to do with 2–4 from a risk management perspective. Yes, we might have to respect quotas or tariffs, but we're complying (or risking wrath). Where life gets trickier is with embargoes. If you're manufacturing the clothing I briefly mentioned, you might get requests from angsty retailers concerned about boycotts and backlashes. The store owners might ask you to fill out lengthy forms listing your suppliers (and sub-suppliers) and attesting that there are no human rights or sanctions violations in your supply chain. Most people will just say yes and hope for the best. In my experience, many mega-corporations don't fully understand the origins of inputs into their supply chain. As data and access to information improve, the ostrich tactic may not help much.

What Should I Do About Sanctions?

The first step is to ask some of my favourite types of questions:

1. **Who:** Does the country (countries) in which you operate maintain a sanctions regime?

2. **Who too:** Do other countries where you source or sell maintain sanctions or controls?

3. **What:** Does what you do attract sanctions (your sector)?

4. **How much:** If the answer is yes to any of the above, what are the restrictions, tariffs, or non-tariff barriers?

Points 1 and 2 are a bit easier than you'd imagine. The US has been a prominent exponent of economic sanctions. The US Department of the Treasury website includes sanctioned countries, organisations, individuals, and further information about enforcement. There is also a searchable list. The United Nations also imposes sanctions through the Security Council, with details on their website. Similarly, the European Union (EU) maintains sanctions and the details are available – you guessed it – on their site. There are many other countries with their own (consistent or different) sanctions regimes, which you will need to consider reviewing (e.g., non-EU but European Economic Area countries, Australia, and New Zealand).

If you're stuck, get professional help. But for most SMEs, it is generally possible to establish at least a high level of understanding of our potential exposure. Once you're clear, the message for your people is pretty simple:

- Don't trade with embargoed entities or countries.

- Don't deal with the economic resources (cash, property, etc.) of sanctioned entities or individuals.

- Don't help them (indirectly or directly), for example, using countries where sanctions don't apply to allow them to access their funds.

- Don't violate trade restrictions, tariffs or quotas.

I appreciate that the application may be more complex, especially for the last point. But much as with conflicts of interest, we want to encourage a disclosure culture where people raise their hands if they're unsure.

If you face potential sanctions risks, invest in training (and reporting lines to escalate concerns or queries). You'll also need to start conducting due diligence and maintaining meticulous records. I'll get on to due diligence in more detail soon.

More generally, sanctions expose the best and worst of our globally connected world. If you examine your value chain and recognise potential risks, there may be no easy options. But that doesn't mean you give up. I collaborate with a business that helps SMEs (and larger firms) identify sustainable and locally sourced alternatives when your current suppliers are no longer an option. There is always a way, and it can spur new opportunities and improve your market positioning. If your sales or users might be (or suddenly are) subject to sanctions, that's bad, but it's survivable.

Anti-Money Laundering

Anti-money laundering (AML) and its cousin, counter-terrorism financing (CTF), are big deals for financial institutions, professional advisors (lawyers, accountants, tax advisors, auditors, etc.), real estate firms, casinos, corporate secretarial companies, and money transmitters. If you operate in those sectors, you might be subject to stringent laws and regulations with extraterritorial reach. But it's not just that list that needs to worry about AML – the scope is expanding. But first, let's look at the background.

The de facto trend-setter in AML and CTF is the Financial Action Task Force (FATF), formed in 1989 at the G7 Paris meeting, which provides a list of recommendations to manage AML. The European Commission has issued directives in line with FATF requirements. Between 2001 and 2004, as the US *Global War on*

Terror took hold, the UK, the US, and the EU authorities, among others, released recommendations, legislation, and guidance strengthening AML provisions, focusing on CTF.

CTF is a subset of AML, focusing on the specific offences of fundraising for terrorist groups or activities, using the money for terrorist purposes, and involvement in arrangements that make money available for terrorist purposes. The issue is the same – stopping the wrong people from using you to transfer or transact their cash.

AML and CTF are big, scary, and include many intimidating acronyms.

Now You See It, Now You Don't

The official definition for money laundering might go something like any act or attempt to disguise the sources of money or assets derived from criminal activity. For CTF, we're more concerned about the destination of the funds. Or, using the prism of my daughter, *making baddies' stuff look legit*. Baddies differ (as we learned in sanctions). You need to understand if you're subject to the long arm of all those acronyms (FATF, EU, etc.). Once that's clear, they publish definitions or lists of those they consider baddies – organised criminals, designated terrorist groups, sanctioned persons, etc.

What we consider baddies' *stuff* is expansive. In the early 2000s, I was mainly concerned with money and property. As the variably gotten gains of the former Soviet Union flooded into the banks of London, my colleagues and I fixated on even more acronyms:

- PEPs – politically exposed persons: politicians, public officials, and their (often extended) family. Why PEPs? Because political folk are involved in corruption and constantly seek to clean the illegal proceeds through legitimate financial instruments.

- UBO – ultimate beneficial ownership; who owns the stuff (companies, property, assets) after you've hit umpteen offshore walls of secrecy, trusts, nominees, and SPVs (special purpose vehicles).

- KYC – know your customer, making sure you understand who you're dealing with (PEPs, UBO, etc.).

- SARs – suspicious activity reports (or STRs, suspicious transaction reports); the notifications you're meant to send to the regulators if you suspect baddies or PEPs are the UBO of the stuff.

Confused? Yeah, I was too. And I was an investigator looking into these (and other) issues. I also went on mind-numbingly dull courses all about this. But it gets worse. We must also contend with an ever-expanding universe of stuff AND trade-based money laundering (TBML). The broadening assets include all the digital ones (crypto to NFTs), expensive items (e.g., designer goods) and progressively more complex financial instruments. Let's deal with the financial (not plain vanilla) baddy stuff first. How does it happen?

1. **Placement** – getting dirty money into the financial system. Often uses *smurfing* (where *smurfs* – not small blue people but no-namers – make deposits below the thresholds that trigger background checks). The smurfs work for the baddies.

2. **Layering** – separating the money from its source, usually using offshore accounts and below-limits movements of capital.

3. **Integration** – investing in physical stuff (property, art, vehicles, etc.), so the baddy can take ownership of this legitimate property.

You can now see why those captured by money laundering extend so broadly to advisors, agents, and brokers facilitating transactions. Before discussing what we need to do to prevent money laundering, it's worth unpicking TBML.

TBML should be a wake-up call for those of us moving products around. The primary mechanisms include manipulating invoices. For instance, if an exporter submits inflated, deflated, or multiple invoices (for the same shipment) to an importer. The inflated (or multiple) invoices create a payment that exceeds the shipment value – benefitting the exporter. Deflated invoices see the greater value transferred from exporter to importer. Another way the importer might benefit is if the exporter ships more goods than agreed (the reverse can also happen). Finally, the value of goods can be misrepresented or misstated (e.g., saying they are of higher quality than is the case).

We've even seen money laundering using rotting fruit and manky old potatoes. The mechanisms can be confusing, and the flow of who gets what is dizzying, but the trick is to remember there is a cost to cleaning money, and one person has the dirty laundry, while the other charges a toll for the cleaning. Focusing on this dynamic (the flow of benefit) should be easier to identify any outlier or unusual transactions.

This cost of cleaning is best demonstrated with designer handbags. I spoke to an organisation in Hong Kong that had seen an initially welcome spike in sales. But alarm bells soon went off. Smurfs would buy as many handbags as they could carry, using cash (or sometimes multiple credit cards) to pay. The bags retailed in thousands of dollars. These bags were smuggled from HK to mainland China and sold on the *nearly new* or *good-as-new* market. For organised criminals, paying $10,000 for a bag or two you sell a few days later for $8,000 (or less) represented the laundry cost. Call it the baddy tax.

Avoiding Rotten Apples and Mouldy Potatoes

The controls required for AML and CTF overlap considerably with ABAC and sanctions, and much of it focuses on understanding who you're dealing with and what they do for you. Some people (including the Basel Institute of Governance's AML Index) rank and assess countries depending on their (non-)compliance with AML requirements. Be alert if you're transacting in or with these places – as we discussed earlier with the North Korean pachinko funds routed through Cambodia.

The trick to managing AML and CTF is to ask questions. That sounds basic. But not knowing who you're dealing with or failing to act on suspicious trades and transactions is terrible business. If things go wrong, you have little recourse, and I'm not just talking AML and CTF. Opacity is where fraud lives. For financial institutions, including FinTech disruptors, you will need to go deep into this, well beyond the scope of this book. The one titbit I should mention before we move on to TBML controls: most regulations require you to disclose suspicious activity (STRs), often through a designated Money Laundering Reporting Officer (MLRO), so check if that's you!

For TBML, much will depend on what it is you do. These questions should help:

1. **Point of transaction:** Is there time to check the purchaser/supplier? Do you know the end customers?

2. **Value:** Do the items have relatively high resale value (as a percentage of the purchase price)? Or can they be repaired/repurposed such that they do?

3. **Measurement:** Are the items easy to over- or understate in sales and shipments? Misstatement of large amounts of goods is hard to check, which explains why food items or smaller items can be appealing. Similarly, anywhere customer traffic can be manipulated will often appeal – food and beverage, salons, gaming parlours, online gaming, and yes, laundromats.

4. **Third-party management:** Are detection tools working to identify issues like ghost suppliers, inflated invoices, and duplicate bills?

5. **Regulatory scrutiny:** Are the items on the radar of the authorities? The regulators can provide helpful guidance on sector-specific issues and what to watch.

These questions should help you narrow your focus to any areas of your operations where you might be vulnerable. You can also take the approach of data analytics and transaction testing to understand the extant threat. It will not be intuitive for most of us. Frontload your prevention budget on training and communication. Your employees are the first line of defence. They need to know where and when to ask questions. Beyond the education and reminding piece, you will need the usual mechanisms (reporting channels, investigative capacity, policies, monitoring tools) and a strong focus on due diligence, particularly CDD (customer due diligence, the new KYC). Welcome to alphabet spaghetti!

Due Diligence: Why and How

KYC, CDD, EDD (enhanced), IDD (integrity), and background checks are all the same: knowing who you're dealing with. I transitioned from counter-terrorism and crisis response into investigations via an excruciating period of doing background checks for financial institutions. It was an excellent education in the world of the baddy. I just didn't appreciate it until much later. I learned how few (good) questions we ask of people we often rely on and to whom we entrust significant sums of money. Background checks can be very daunting, especially for those with limited resources. I want to see how we can change that.

The most direct parallel is online dating (given how many organisations transact remotely). A year or two back, we did a poster campaign to raise awareness around third-party risks using the Tinder swipe-right concept. For those pretending not to know what Tinder is, it's a dating app where you swipe right on profiles you want to match with and left on those you'd rather avoid.

If we break down the parallel into a few steps, the similarities become more apparent – the seven steps to heaven or hell.

1. **Who is this person?:** You run an image search for their profile photo and find it linked to an Italian underwear model. You're speaking to someone in Nantucket. We rely on similar research in the corporate world but couple this with watchlist checks to rule out obvious charlatans and shysters.

2. **We dream the same dreams:** Do you want the same things? You're considering marriage material, and your match opens the chat asking for bank details. In organisational terms, third parties obsessed with the transaction and wanting minimal interaction beyond that should be an immediate red flag.

3. **Track record and transparency:** Your match claims to be the CEO of a tech startup and talks about their loft apartment. In the background of their photos, you spot a single bed, Baywatch memorabilia, an inflatable doll, and marijuana leaf posters. We might consider reference checks, case studies, or other evidence of past performance. For significant (and long-term) deals, we might also need transparency around financial performance, capacity, and resources.

4. **Skeletons:** They ask to meet for dinner at 5 p.m. in a dimly lit diner with no obvious CCTV. You're distracted by a blinking red light on their ankle tag, shining through the fire hazard joggers. Many organisations have had ethical issues – ranging from minor disputes to more serious criminal prosecutions, boycotts, and sustained adverse publicity. We need to know the backstory to decide whether this represents an ongoing liability or if there's evidence of improvement.

5. **Catfish:** You can't find your date in the bar and are unnerved by the person on the booster seat with the wine nose dribbling as they leer at the server. They look nothing like the

photos, more mastiff than matinee idol. It's not just social media denizens who've mastered lighting, angles, and touch-up apps. Many businesses are adroit at presenting a slick and professional (online) presence. For more significant deals, you will probably need a site visit to kick some tyres (or get someone else to do it).

6. **Values:** You love children and dogs; your match calls children hell-hobbits and keeps tarantulas. I appreciate that values may seem a nice optional extra for many organisational interactions. But it's essential in longer-term partnerships that there are some alignments, especially around ethical expectations.

7. **A meeting of equals:** You tell them you're a paediatrician; they reply, "Isn't that illegal?" You don't have to be of similar professional competencies to form an ethically sound relationship. It helps to speak the same language, especially around risk. If they talk a good game but can't name a single control or risk process, that's a worry.

These examples may seem glib, but they're not. We make terrible organisational dating decisions when under pressure or unaware of risks. I was discussing third-party risk with an engineer recently, and they explained a recent close call. Their firm needed a part for a specialised machine, and fast. They found one on eBay with a London-listed seller. Leveraging a generous corporate credit card limit, the engineer bought the expensive item without guarantees. Luckily it arrived on the other side of the world a week later. The shipping label was from Turkey. Turkey has a solid manufacturing base. It also shares borders with Syria and Iraq, where human exploitation of refugee populations by unscrupulous enterprises is a challenge, let alone corruption and money laundering.

The transact quick, ask (no) questions later approach is more the norm than the exception. Sometimes you'll get away with it. Or it ends in disaster. There is much that can go awry by working with the wrong people – every violation in this book. At the risk of labouring the point, the law (in most cases) does not distinguish between acts you commit and those commissioned on your behalf. As societal mores evolve, consumers and broader stakeholders don't care either. So what if it is a sub-sub-supplier who runs the sweatshop? You're the one selling the T-shirts. Who cares that an unqualified but outsourced maintenance contractor caused the toxic sludge to seep into riverways?

To avoid these perils, we must prioritise. In the example I gave about my business's interactions with third parties, not all of them posed a threat related to bribery and corruption. That doesn't mean I don't need to know anything more. Bribery is just one risk. If your risk assessment has worked well, you'll have a decent understanding of potential exposure to your operations. If you haven't done the risk assessment yet, here is a quick and dirty hack: what are your crown jewels? For most of us, this is a blend of what we do (our core offering) and our greatest assets (people, intellectual property, goodwill, reputation, money, market share, whatever works for you).

How might those third parties you deal with ruin, tarnish, steal, or compromise your crown jewels? First, we must look at what most people do and then do the opposite.

What Not To Do

Since starting my own business, I've filled out many *vendor onboarding questionnaires*. It's a study in Kafka-style bureaucracy that is its own satire. So repetitious and pointless are most of the questions that I've created an Excel file so I can copy and paste for the next batch. What's driving this process for process's sake? I don't know, but my working theories are:

- **Case law curse:** Each time a new regulation or law comes out, we just bolt on more questions rather than ask if they're duplicative of existing ones.

- **CYA:** Cover Your Ass. We add it, just in case, rather than consider if a question is relevant.

- **NMJ:** Not My Job. The poor souls we ask to trawl through these forms regret the cards life has dealt them and are stuck in dead-end roles, so there's little incentive to innovate or take on the additional work of fixing the mess.

We use hefty forms that *vendors* skim through, ticking all the right boxes and moving on. It's like those terms and conditions we get on our phones when they update the software; it's too long to read and too dense to understand, so we click "accept". If you query any of the questions and clauses – as I mistakenly do – you limit your chances of selection and delay projects and payment.

Some will hail technology as the saviour, but not unless the structural and ideological deficiencies are addressed first; rubbish in, rubbish out.

How Do We Get Out?

Armed with our risk assessment and values – or at least an understanding of our crown jewels – we should know what risks we want to avoid. We calibrate our Tinder checklist.

Some of that information might be hard to obtain. For example, confirming someone's exact identity (remember ultimate beneficial ownership?) without reliable and easily accessible global registries is incredibly hard. I appreciate that you'll need to default to processes and automation for some organisations – like massive e-commerce platforms with a gazillion vendors. But for those of us whose third-party universe remains in the hundreds (even low thousands), start simple and build complexity only when you absolutely must. For example, ask questions around:

1. Location and sector – simple dropdowns with limited choices (some sector code lists run into the hundreds, avoid this). Using the selections should create a composite risk score on the back-end of whatever system (or spreadsheet).

2. Consider how to respond to issues – if you get a hit on a watchlist (let's say a business partner is a PEP), so what? If your logistics provider was implicated in a fraud on the other side of the world three years ago, does that mean you cancel the contract? Figure 6.3 was my first attempt at a process flow to help organisations contextualise these issues.

3. Conflict checks, payment terms, and reliance risk are ideally automated, but you'll often still need a few binary questions with risk weighting attached. For conflicts, that might include:

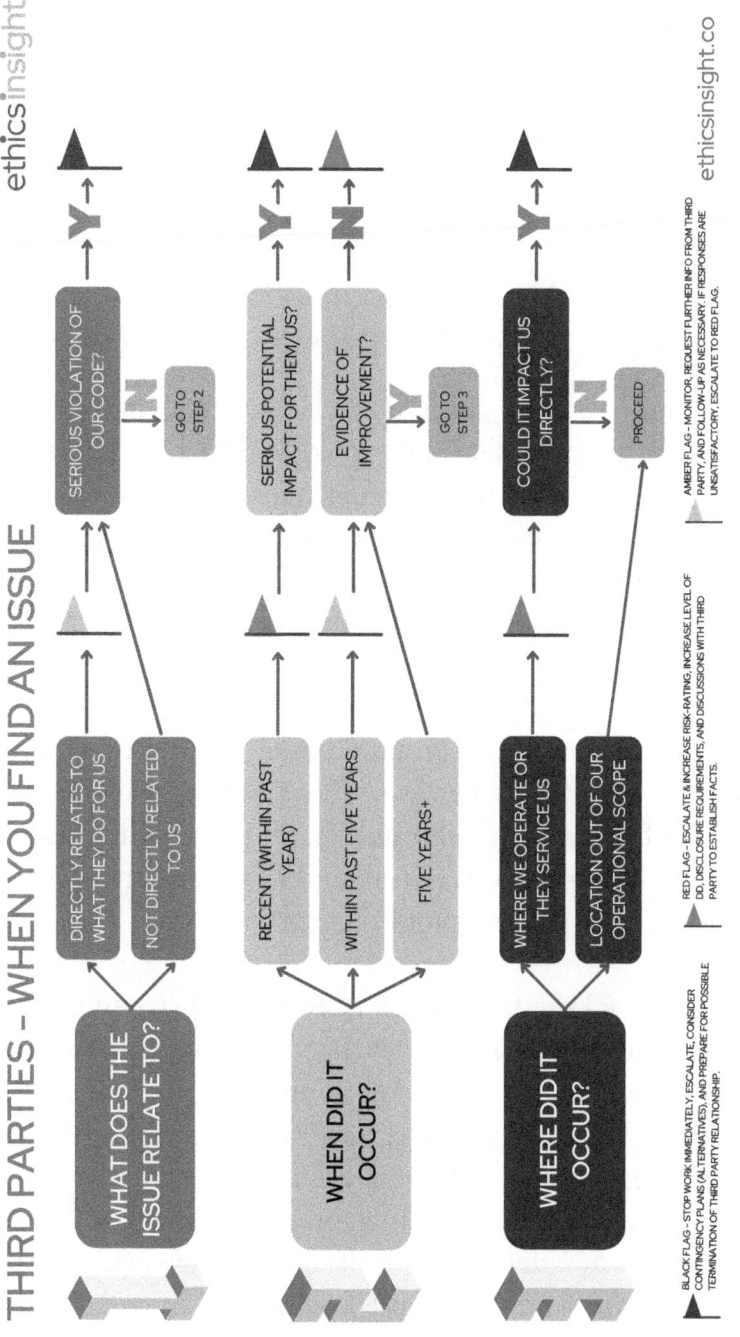

Figure 6.3 Third parties – when you find an issue.

a. Are we aware of any close personal relationships between the third party and our employees?

b. Are any of the third party's key personnel our former employees?

c. Was the third party introduced to us by a current or former employee?

d. Did a government official introduce the third party?

4. Values and maturity risk is a real challenge to automate. Let's say the third party shares their Code. So what? Enron had a Code. If you're unable (time, resources, access) to look under the bonnet and assess how the compliance engine runs, being sent a photo of the vehicle doesn't help you decide whether it's a reliable runner or a liability. Best to only ask for high-risk and long-term partnerships.

If you get a simple ranking process, the human inputs should sit at decision points (i.e., when you find a risk issue). The trick is striking that balance between caution and not flooding decision-makers with false positives. Tweak and adapt any rating weightings as you go; the process should not be static.

The decision-making framework in Figure 6.3 (when you identify a third-party issue) illustrates that people need to know why we ask what we do. As risks love company, it can also help to take a step back. Don't get lost in the different categories – fraud, bribery, conflicts of interest, money laundering, sanctions, environmental degradation, human rights, etc. Recognise that they look similar from a detection point of view. I picked on ABAC, AML/CTF, trade sanctions, and human rights and looked at potential third-party red flags. There is more similarity than dissonance (Figure 6.4).

Outsourcing: Smoke and Bullshit

If this all looks too excruciatingly painful, I do sympathise. Risk-ranking your third parties and then vetting the higher-risk ones are hard work. Research may be impossible, for example, if your new partner is based in a country where you (and your associates) don't speak the language, how can you conduct a proper background check? Is it even worth doing that work in places where you can't check the disclosure – like countries with heavily censored media or where corporate data requires local retrieval?

If you give up and outsource, there are plenty of screening and due diligence providers. Some will tout a data-led approach, citing unique algorithms or proprietary databases that map connections. You might even get a demo reminiscent of one of those spy movies where they can scan a face in seconds and geolocate the person instantly with a drone conveniently hovering above and with no bad weather. Be careful.

A couple of excellent firms have invested decades in building a map of international dirtbags. Sometimes, the interface they sell you resembles a travel booking system in the early 2000s (for youthful readers, it has the same functionality as the "Hello world" app you built in year six). I hope disruptors will continue to challenge the status quo, and I think blockchain has potential, especially when it comes to accurately representing the origin of inputs (funds for AML, supply chain origins for environmental and human rights screening, for starters).

THIRD-PARTY RED FLAGS

TOPIC	ABAC	AML / CTF	SANCTIONS	HUMAN RIGHTS
Unclear why they're being considered/proposed	☒	☒	☒	☒
Unclear beneficial ownership/ complex offshore structures	☒	☒	☒	?
Lack of experience, resources or staff for proposed engagement	☒	☒	☒	?
Relies heavily on government connections	☒	☒	?	?
Unable to adequately explain supply chain inputs	?	☒	☒	☒
Request for unusual transaction terms/routes	☒	☒	☒	☒
Relies on outsourcing (e.g., subcontractors)	☒	☐	☒	☒
Appears 'intangible' (little website/physical presence)	☒	☒	☒	☒
Unable or unwilling to disclose origins of wealth	☒	☒	☒	?
Refuses to accept compliance clauses in contract	☒	☒	☒	☒

ethicsinsight.co ethicsinsight

Figure 6.4 Third-party red flags.

In major deals, especially significant investments, market-entry, mergers and acquisitions, you might decide to splurge on a due diligence (DD) provider conducting source enquiries (sometimes glamorously called HUMINT – human intelligence). I built a network of assets (informants, sources, stringers, human intelligence) across many countries to help with broader intelligence gathering efforts and some DD. When done well, the information you can find about people is staggering, which can be the difference between success and failure. When not done well, it's a joke. Unfortunately, most DD providers aren't very diligent, there's the irony. They will generally maintain a stable of contacts and spam them with the names of your proposed partner. It's that basic.

Let me give you an example. A beverage firm was trying to understand if three senior members of their distributor in Malaysia (all ethnic Chinese) were defrauding the firm. The DD report I received started with, "None of our sources confirmed the allegations, and we found no evidence of wrongdoing." As I read, these sources were revealed in vagaries (usually the case), with lines like, "No one at the Chinese Chamber of Commerce has heard of them." As I speak DD, I know what happened here. The provider has assets in the chamber of commerce, feeding them gossip on members. Just because our trio of possible fraudsters hadn't come across this person's radar, that was considered evidence of their low profile. The logic baffled me. Like, we asked a man in a pub if he'd seen Subject A murder Subject B. He confirmed he had not. Therefore, Subject A is likely innocent.

A proper investigations outfit would do some work. Do their lifestyles match their income? Do they (or, more likely, friends and family) hold other corporate interests? Where is the stolen booze sold, and can we arrange a test purchase (to confirm the seller)?

The easiest way to spot the pros from the clowns is to ask them about their sources. If you get flannelled with a chat about their extensive and top-secret network, you're speaking to a joker. If they explain possible avenues of enquiry and the benefits and limitations of each (usually a trade-off between discretion and depth), you're talking to a pro. The pro won't burn their sources and tell you exactly who they are, but they can tell you about their access, background and proximity to the subjects of the enquiry.

Logical Deduction

Bringing these strands together to bootstrap a third-party risk management framework, I'd do this:

1. Use your risk profile, appetite, and values to define what and who you don't want to partner with.

2. Consider what indicators you'd need to determine this, starting with the publicly available data, disclosure information (from the third party), and any gaps you may need to plug with further enquiries.

3. Develop a simple risk-ranking questionnaire with logic in the questions (i.e., if a *yes* response increases risk, you may want to ask further questions that you shouldn't inflict on someone answering *no*).

4. Invest in an online system that is simple and customisable (easily) – often, you may need to dovetail with procurement and contract management programs.

5. Educate and arm the people reviewing (often procurement) with simple cheat sheets and memory aids so they know *why* you're asking these questions and *who* to flag.

6. Tweak the steps above until you're starting to eliminate the false positives.

7. Pray that blockchain, artificial intelligence, or something saves us all from these processes.

Monitoring, Ethically

Once you're working with people – third parties, clients, employees – we're faced with a new set of complex problems. What and who should we monitor? For some, that will include monitoring the implementation of specific regulations and guidelines. For others, it will focus on measuring the gap between awareness of your expectations and adherence.

An example of the first category (regulation), AML laws require financial institutions (and others) to monitor transactions, looking for unusual patterns or deviations. For example, if a largely dormant account starts transferring US$9,999 regularly into overseas accounts. Sadly, it won't be that easy, but you get the gist.

Beyond these regulated areas, where should you start and stop? Yes, you've guessed it. It depends on what you do, your risk appetite, and who you want to be.

- **Establish a baseline:** If you assess behaviour compared to expected behaviour, what you expect must be clear. Make sure it is. Monitor and evaluate the understanding, access and trust, as discussed in Chapter 2.

- **Make it measurable:** The more you can make your findings measurable, the easier it is for others to understand, for you to observe trends, and for you to compare over time. To do this, you may need to keep consistent datasets.

- **Make it easy:** Colleagues (and third parties) do not often welcome monitoring and audits. Keep interviews, information requests, and questionnaires as simple as possible. Check if anyone else has scheduled audits and when their busy periods are.

- **Always look for lessons:** Be open to feedback and suggestions. Look for possible case studies and lessons for others in your findings. We learn most and respond positively to examples relevant to what we do. Use the monitoring as an opportunity to develop communication and training content.

Let's use a couple of monitoring hypotheticals borrowed from the hairnet CCTV fiasco investigation I discussed in Chapter 2. You run an e-commerce business in two parallel universes and regularly conduct ad-hoc audits (to keep them unpredictable).

In Orwellverse (the first parallel universe), you rely on CCTV and stop-searches by security guards at the facility gate. You conduct screening due diligence on employees, requiring they consent to criminal record and bankruptcy checks. Your employees aren't much enamoured with any of your processes, feeling the CCTV in the breakout room and changing rooms is a bit much. When you discover the theft of smartphones, you hire an investigations firm that spends hours (and thousands of dollars) watching CCTV footage. The investigators spot plenty of theft but struggle to identify any culprits as the CCTV is ceiling-mounted and shows only people wearing white hairnets and hats (your uniform). Familiar, huh?!

In Betterverse, you've worked out what your crown jewels are – the valuable items people might want to pinch or otherwise fraudulently manipulate. This analysis helps you focus your monitoring less on people and more on the flow of stock through the system – purchasing volumes, delivery, quality control, storage, retrieval once ordered, packing, and dispatch. At each gateway, you have scanners for the stocktaking and spot checks (to keep the packaging intact). You maintain job rotation policies so no one stays on one station long enough to get crushingly bored (and do serious fraudulent damage). Your CCTV has a good line-of-sight but is limited to packing stations, delivery, and dispatch. Your systems flag a discrepancy in the scans of smartphones when they're dispatched, and you can intervene before the fraud takes root.

Life is never as simple as these scenarios. In Orwellverse, we were monitoring people. Yes, it might still be good practice to conduct screening, and certain high-risk functions will need more scrutiny, but it's usually more efficient to ensure your monitoring is risk-led, not profiling people. There are many positive reasons to avoid profiling – including ethical ones – but it's also a waste of time and money. The small percentage of people with ill intent in any population will soon wise up to your tactics and start using people who don't fit your profiles.

Take a risk-based approach instead. Identify your crown jewels, and consider *how* they might come to harm, not *who* might do it. Build your monitoring around higher-risk areas and behaviours and pick the right tools for the job. There are numerous such tools, and rather than list them, next time you go to a place of work, count the cameras, access points, registrations, logins, passwords, and keycard swipes. When we add on the decision and approval nodes on anything money-related – approvals, purchase orders, customer details – you will soon realise that you have a universe of data to monitor, making it a Betterverse.

A school of thought suggests that publicising your monitoring activities reduces risk and increases the perception of detection. Again, I'd look at who you are and your values as an organisation. I worked in some roles – including counter-espionage ones – where I expected to be subject to enhanced scrutiny. It made sense, and I accepted it comes with the territory. I felt differently when I was a lowly intern in a glacially slow communications role and my employer published internet usage data, naming and shaming the top 10 loafers. I never made it onto that illustrious list. I tried. Hard. But it struck me as a pretty rubbish thing to be monitoring in an early-stage e-commerce business.

Endnotes

1. There may be some national and sectoral rules to which you will need to pay particular attention. For example, after corruption and price-fixing scandals in the healthcare sector, some domestic enforcers now have laws that require you to record and report all payments you make to healthcare professionals.
2. If you're wondering how to work out the most important laws, any game-changers, law firms, and other advisors will widely publicise any regulatory updates and enhancements. Setting up a few email alerts (relevant to what you do) will generally be enough (certainly in the SME space) to stay updated.

7
PROTECTING YOUR HOME

I used to think fraud was mainly concerned with mispresenting – unscrupulous types posing as salespeople and defrauding friendly pensioners. Stories I'd see in the local news as a kid. I was wrong. Fraud is a massive area of risk encompassing many topics we've covered, like bribery, money laundering, and conflicts of interest. In each of these topics, there's a significant *demand-side* external risk. This chapter is more concerned with the assets and threats within – employees and other stakeholders intentionally or unintentionally subverting your controls, enabling fraud and data loss. How might we protect our organisation's precious contents and data?

The Universe of Fraud

Fraud is wrongful or criminal deception intended to result in financial or personal gain. A non-exhaustive list (with topics already covered removed) would look like Table 7.1.

You can see how conflicts of interest, anti-competition, insider trading, kickbacks, bribes and the rest would slot nicely under some of these headings. I suppose I could have called this chapter Miscellaneous as it is a catch-all for integrity risks we've not yet covered.

Table 7.1 Examples of fraud

Type of fraud	Examples
Asset misappropriation	• Wrongful use or acquiring of money, supplies or other assets • Destruction, removal, or inappropriate use of assets
Reporting and false declarations	• Misreporting or mishandling money or financial transactions, including accounts receivable fraud • Misrepresentation of financial statements and reporting • Fake documents in loan applications, expense claims, or invoices
Misuse of information	• Data theft, including trade secrets, personal data, and customer data
Third-party fraud	• Billing schemes, including fake vendors, invoices, and price-fixing
Payroll fraud	• Ghost employee schemes, expenses fraud, and timesheet fraud
Counterfeit	• Product substitution, tampering, grey market activities or counterfeit

At the beginning of the book, I mentioned the 2–5% estimates cited in various studies quantifying the cost of fraud. Would 2% more funding, revenue, or budget help? Of course! Let's refresh a few concepts brought up in those first chapters to see how we might do that.

The Behavioural Approach

Remember opportunity, pressure (or need) and rationalisation (the fraud triangle)? We've discussed different tactics to identify weak spots (opportunity). Risk assessment, monitoring, due diligence, analytics, and other screening techniques and tools will help. If that's not (yet) feasible, we should look to counter-terrorism. When trying to prevent terrorist incidents, we need to do an equation:

$$\text{Intent} - (\text{your vulnerability} + \text{predictability}) - \text{capability} = \text{threat level}$$

- **Threat intent:** What might terrorists want to target?

- **Security vulnerability:** How physically (and electronically) secure are those targets?

- **Predictability vulnerability:** How predictable is our security?

- **Threat capability:** How capable are the terrorists of overcoming our defences?

Whatever the terminology, the framework works for fraud. Figure 7.1 is a non-scientific mock-up of how you might plot a few different fraud risks considering your typical fraudster.

I still use this model, which helped me transition from counter-terrorism into investigative roles. By distilling rationalisation and pressure, we can flesh out the *intent* part. Terrorists are sometimes helpful – publishing their intent and the rationalisations. We're not so lucky when looking at integrity risk. I'd broadly split fraudulent decisions into two camps:

1. I was doing it for you.

2. I was doing it for me.

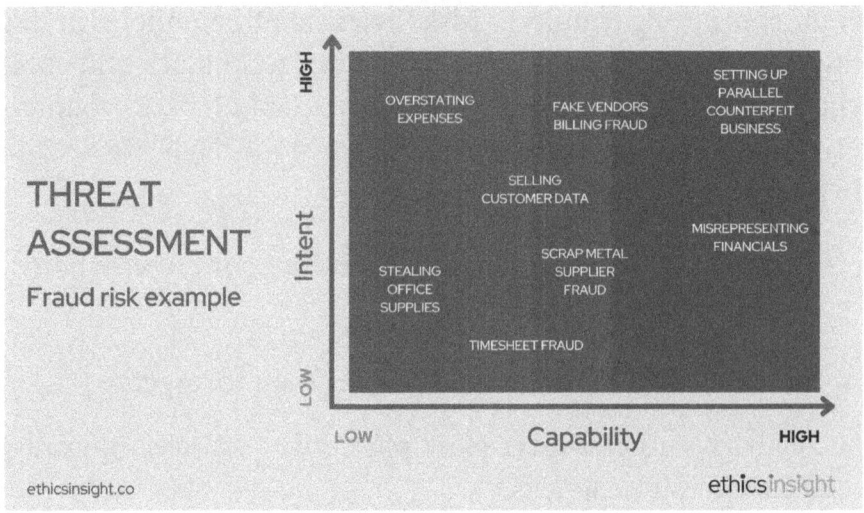

Figure 7.1 Threat assessment: intent and capability.

When people think they're doing your organisation a favour, you'll hear the ethical excuses (rationalisation) from the bingo game in Chapter 5. They won't tell you their motives or justifications if they're trying to dupe you for personal gain. We need to blend the models to get better results. Picking three cases, I worked on and briefly analysing them should help demonstrate how to do this:

- **Asset misappropriation:** A supervisor at a manufacturing facility oversees the scrapping of waste and defective parts (*opportunity*). Their pay is low, the work is hard, and the company is doing well ("they can afford it", *rationalisation*). The scrap amounts and value fluctuate, and this non-core activity has minimal oversight (*vulnerability*). The supervisor knows the company's tolerance for defective parts and conspires with the scrap dealer to *write off* good parts as faulty (*capability*). This scam nets the supervisor $100,000 (*pressure; need*).

- **Misuse of information:** A manager in an overseas business process outsourcing (BPO) facility for a major multinational has access to sensitive data about US government employees (*opportunity*). They hear of pending redundancies (*rationalisation*) and use their managerial access privileges (*capability*) to steal significant amounts of information from poorly secured systems (*vulnerability*). The manager tries to extort their employer for some cash and name the people they want to be spared from the redundancies (*pressure*). It doesn't end well once the local SWAT team get involved.

- **Payroll fraud:** An HR director has oversight of employee data for a whole region (*opportunity*). The director sets up two unsuccessful candidates as employees (*capability*) in a system without analytics monitoring employee address and bank account overlap (*vulnerability*). The ghost employees' salary goes into the director's bank account (*pressure; need*). We never established rationalisation, as they fled the region with the net closing in.

I appreciate that, in retrospect, it is easy to look at the indicators and reasons. Maybe then, I should try and summarise some of the critical areas. Table 7.2 will never be a complete anti-fraud plan, but it should help you scan through and see what (if anything) you're not currently doing (well). The weighting and utility of each element will depend on what you do and how you do it.

You'll be familiar with many of these areas, but lifestyle analysis and behavioural indicators may jump out.

Table 7.2 Anti-fraud plan

Opportunity (security)	Intent (pressure and rationalisation)	Capability: predictability
• Risk assessment • Policies and procedures • Screening (employees and third parties) • Analytics • Investigative capacity • Financial, electronic, and physical controls • Reporting lines (speak-up effectiveness)	• Psychological safety data • Employee engagement information • Lifestyle analysis • Behavioural indicators • Incentives and disciplinary measures (enforcement consistency) • Management oversight	• Random checks (audits, testing, analytics) • Process controls (think of the monitoring at the factory in Chapter 6) • Segregation of duties, access, and job rotation • Risk-based monitoring

Lifestyle Analysis

What's going on in the personal lives of your people? Do you think you have a right to know? Do you even want to know? It's a tricky topic in the era of surveillance and increased blurring of personal and professional. If you think back to the conflicts of interest examples in Chapter 4, the intersection of those two realms can be a mess. The anti-fraud purists may tell you to focus on three potential indicators of increased risk:

1. Living beyond means.

2. Financial difficulties.

3. Family problems.

It's not a massive leap of imagination to see why an admin assistant turning up to work in a $150,000 sports car might raise eyebrows and concerns. Similarly, Chapter 4 discussed how financial challenges might create pressure to generate alternative income streams when we looked at side hustles. Family problems might include divorce, legal problems, bailing relatives out of their failed businesses, your partner losing their job, and myriad other issues. There are some considerable ethical challenges when it comes to lifestyle analysis, including:

1. **Who** has the capacity and the skills to look out for indicators of lifestyle issues gracefully and appropriately? Please don't say "line managers"; few are comfortable or qualified to conduct lifestyle profiling.

2. **What** is an indicator? Without granular insight, we might see the $150,000 sports car and leap into action, failing to recognise that the assistant's sibling is a tech millionaire who gifted them the car they'd always wanted.

3. If we spot an indicator, **how** might we proceed? Surveillance? An invasive and awkward chat about "trouble at home"?

4. **Why** do we even want to get into this territory?

I'd defer to the type of organisation you are and your values. Couple that with a suitable risk assessment to identify where you might be vulnerable, add a pinch of unpredictable monitoring, and build a robust speak-up culture. But that's me. I've had this discussion with others in the field, and they prefer adopting an attitude of professional scepticism. That makes sense if you're a risk manager, internal auditor, investigator, or another function where your job is to sniff out wrongdoing. If you're more a counsellor than an enforcer, focus on building cultures where people can share problems before they become chronic.

If you decide to include lifestyle analysis in your anti-fraud toolkit, please make it risk-based and consider alternative hypotheses if you find *smoke*. I've investigated would-be fraudsters' lifestyles (and asset profiles), which often generate even more smoke. The fire is, and always will be, your assets exiting your organisation – start there.

Behavioural Indicators

What do people's work behaviours say about the fraud risk they pose? When discussing discrimination and harassment in Chapter 3, I mentioned how toxic cultures increase fraud risks. If the people at the top can get away with treating people poorly, they'll unlikely stop there. The data (from the ACFE surveys) also tells us that senior employees' frauds are the costliest – not a huge surprise. They have access, approvals, and experience. Your monitoring should always cover the top.

As the funnel opens to middle management and more junior employees, we need to consider proximity to third parties, not taking due leave, defensiveness, a lack of sharing, and bullying. If you're up to no good, taking time off increases the chances someone else will find out (as they cover your work). Similarly, if you're colluding with suppliers, you will want to keep others out of those dealings. As people ask questions, continued evasion may be challenging, leading to defensive of bullying responses. You get the idea that if employees behave like surly teenagers (hiding, not sharing, or responding defensively), be alert.

How might we avoid these issues? Luckily for you, we've already discussed job rotation, segregation of duties, team access rights, monitoring, analytics, and other deterrents (training, reporting lines, audits, etc.). Focus on an intelligence-led approach to fraud prevention rather than create cultures of suspicion, surveillance, and (amateur) psychological profiling.

Data Privacy

Leaks of personal or organisational data can attract significant negative publicity and impact the trust customers and stakeholders have in your organisation. The definition of personal data, protection and retention periods differs across countries. The first step, talk to a specialist. Data privacy is not an area where I'd advocate winging it. For example, the EU's General Data Protection Regulation (GDPR) extends beyond the data you can hold to cover the export of that information outside the EU or European Economic Area.

Putting on my integrity risk hat – and sidestepping the technicalities of an area best left to others – let's consider data privacy in the context of ethical issues and what to (not) do.

What Is It?

Broadly, data privacy requires a clear and defensible purpose for collecting people's information (i.e., don't try and collect sensitive personal data for no apparent reason). Once you have their data, you can't share it with others without their consent – or under exceptional circumstances (like a police request related to a possible crime). You can't hold the data longer than needed (often termed "stated purpose"), and it must be accurate and updated. If you're sending the data, be careful about sharing it with places that don't adhere to similar protection standards.

What (Not) to Do

It depends (on where you operate). But we should pick a high bar.

If you have a breach, I know it's scary but don't try and hide it. You will erode trust and destroy integrity. Don't deny individuals access to the data you hold (or their requests that you transfer or delete it). I'm sure you've signed up for some service and seen long policies and tick boxes that take ages to read and bury clauses about sharing your data widely. Don't do that.

If you're holding personal data, you must protect it. Given many security breaches involve human error or involvement, you'll also need to train your people. If you're keeping the circle of people with access to personal data restricted (as you should), you can split the training. Establish a baseline awareness (for everyone) and supplement with tactical guidance for those on the frontline of this issue.

You may have heard of *privacy by design*, which ensures you build your systems and controls with data protection at the core. As someone with a Software as a Service (SaaS) platform, this keeps me up at night. The stomach butterflies intensified as we matured and implemented CRM (customer relationship management) systems. Why? Because most organisations will experience a breach. I'd therefore advocate a less is more approach to data. I don't want any more of your information than I need.

Don't share information across borders without understanding the risks (and without consent). If you're big enough for cross-border issues, you'll likely need a Data Protection Officer and controls to segregate access to data (need-to-know basis only).

Information Security

Your data is of value. Baddies (sometimes termed "hostile actors" in this context) include state-sponsored espionage, competitors, organised criminals and direct-action activists. Their interests in your data differ, but the methods used to steal it remain similar.

The fraud section covered determining what data might interest baddies (intent, pressure, rationalisation). To avoid repetition, we'll focus on information security-centric questions. On operations to counter foreign spies, competitors, criminals and direct-action groups, my role was profiling and identifying the baddies, considering:

1. **What** do you do? Do you have access to (or develop/store) high-value intellectual property, proprietary technology, financial information or sensitive data?

2. Do you operate in locations **where** your data interests hostile actors (for security, political or commercial reasons)?

3. **Who** do you have data on? Are any of them of interest to hostile actors, including health, financial, political, behavioural, and other sensitive personal data?

4. **When** might your exposure change? For example, during competitive commercial situations (tenders, bids), new product development, market-entry, or sensitive negotiations.

You might look at that list and think, doesn't that cover most people? Yes. But we've whittled down the entirety of your information universe to a (hopefully) smaller dataset of possible baddies and potential vulnerabilities.

How It Happens

Much focus is spent on cyber defences but do not discount physical security and social engineering. I'll leave penetration of your technical infrastructure to the pros, which still gives us two-thirds of the risk to work with. Surveys and my anecdotal experience suggest that a physical or social slip-up was to blame in around two-thirds of information security breaches.

I once bluffed my way into a mental health institute, where I gathered information to help secure the release of someone wrongfully detained. I didn't hack the facility – I can barely edit a website. I analysed weak physical security controls – including tailgating at secure doors and not checking photo passes. Breezing through the checkpoints to get to the room I wanted (with the data I needed) was a matter of timing and confidence, acting as if I belonged. It had nothing to do with technology. Get your physical security in order. Don't let people wander around, don't leave sensitive information lying around, and don't leave screens visible. I'm not trying to be glib, but it is that simple. How often have you travelled and seen people working on their laptops or heard loud (but private) conversations?

I enjoy social engineering – gathering sensitive data and trying to stop others from returning the favour. Finding out which of three warring siblings would wrest control of a major state-owned enterprise (accounting for 25% of that country's GDP) isn't a question you can just ask. It's like a puzzle. I would find a cast list of people with answers to micro-questions and then develop a reason for them to ask or answer my questions. We all do this in other forms of life – no judgement here! Sometimes, it might get clever, like the case where a lawyer working on a sensitive merger in a hostile foreign country took some family time. His son won a digital camera at the resort in an art contest and duly plugged the device into his dad's laptop – a data breach aided by social engineering. The competition had been rigged by the hostile state's agents – elaborate yet very simple.

What To Do

You know what's coming by now – it depends on your risk exposure! At a general and very high level, consider:

Cyber defence:

- Focus on **behaviours:** avoid pop-ups, unknown emails and links, and beware of phishing.

- Develop strong **controls:** passwords, multifactor authentication, firewalls, secure Wi-Fi and VPN, quality security systems (regularly updated), back-up files, and look for weak links (Internet of Things).

Data protection:

- **Share less:** exercise caution whenever asked to share information, and do not post material that may reveal any sensitive information (see Data Privacy section).

- **Monitor third parties:** be careful who you allow to access your data and monitor them (often, they will be your weakest link and many hackers know this).

Training and procedures:

- **Training:** help your people identify, respond, and speak up about potential or actual information security breaches.

- **Procedures:** if you identify risks, have systems to manage them (e.g., blocking all USB connections except for approved and encrypted data storage devices).

- **Social engineering:** educate employees on how hostile actors may seek to exploit indiscretion or coerce them.

Physical controls:

- **Security reviews:** review your security and access control regularly, including penetration testing, where you test how easy it is to gain access to your facilities and obtain confidential or sensitive information.

- **Keep clean:** shred documents, clean desk policies, wipe whiteboards, wear passes, shut computers when away from them, etc.

Respond appropriately:

- **Speak up:** if you know or suspect something is wrong, raise it (including if you have been personally compromised).

- **Have contingency plans:** back-up data, know the local threat environment, prepare and test business continuity plans, own up to leaks and maintain and practise dawn raid protocols.

Once again, you'll see several familiar themes: risk assessments, appropriate controls and content, training, guidance that works, and responding appropriately. Risk management isn't that complicated. The architecture looks similar whether we're trying to prevent foreign agents from hacking or employees harassing. Now it's time to bring it all together.

8

KEEPING IT SIMPLE AND COST-EFFECTIVE

Hopefully, the integrity risk universe has come into focus. We've discussed what to do about individual issues throughout. This chapter will bring together overarching themes, models, and ideas. We focus less here on *what* risks and more on *how* to manage them and communicate with and engage your stakeholders without blowing your budget. Usually, this is a conversation, so please contact me if you'd like to discuss anything we cover in more detail. First, let's do a recap.

In Chapter 1, we discussed how (well-chosen) values can form sturdy branches on which to hang our ethical expectations. Purpass, however, will breed cynicism and implode the moral high ground you claim. Remember, we judge ourselves on intentions and others on their actions. Get feedback. We need to know where there's dissonance between aims and actuality.

Chapter 2 outlined the interconnectivity between three risk elements, external environment, internal controls, and culture. Assess and monitor them all. You can build a home without considering the environment and the inhabitants, but you'll misuse the budget and create dissatisfaction. Make sure your incentives reflect, not sidestep, risk. Nurture a speak-up culture; it's a vital reduction tactic. Respond compassionately and professionally to complaints. Ensure you resource investigations appropriately – not an area to go gonzo.

Treat your people (and the planet) fairly, or at least honestly. Chapter 3 made a case for diversity as a risk deterrent. You'll also benefit from creative solutions to knotty problems by including multiple perspectives in decisions. Learn from security and HSE teams; they've been at the inclusion and simplification game longer. Shockingly, discriminating and harassing people create other risks. Don't do it. Protect those brave enough to come forward.

Chapter 4 discussed how work will overlap with our outside interests and loyalties. There will be some hard lines. Define them clearly. Where boundaries blur, encourage a culture of disclosure. You will need trust to do this well. Earn it (using the steps in Chapter 2). Destigmatise conflicts of interest and allow people to unburden their worries.

Chapter 5, giving and receiving, focused on simplification. Subsuming your time answering questions about taxis and tea serves no one. If there's no apparent reason, don't do it. Once the *why* is clear, what, who, and when become more intuitive. Get people to step outside what they *can* do to consider perception.

By Chapter 6, we were in the weeds of integrity risk. Not all will be relevant. If you get your risk assessment right (Chapter 2), you'll focus on protecting your crown jewels; the things that make your organisation survive and thrive. With business partners, trust but verify. Due diligence is essential in higher-risk relationships. It's also a massive waste of money if not risk-based; define what you're (not) looking for in a partner. Monitor third parties and employees proportionately, focusing on risk indicators and behaviours, not clumsy profiling.

In Chapter 7, we surfed the monster wave of fraud and information security. Almost all of us will experience these issues – get to know them. Consider what counter-terrorism can teach us about assessing threat (intent and capability) and our vulnerability (security and predictability). Respond to fraud practically and tactically – a certain proportion of any population will want to defraud you. It will happen. But if you've identified your crown jewels, focused on behaviours, and built that speak-up culture, you can significantly reduce duration and cost.

How might we bring all these strands together? It's as easy as ABC.

The ABC Model

A while back, as Ethics Insight matured, I hired a marketing team to help save me from my uselessness. As Aveline asked me to explain integrity risk management, she said, "Ah, it's an ABC model – assess, build, change." Risk gibberish to relatable risk.

Figure 8.1 summarises the approach. It is an iterative (not always linear) process where you will jump between the elements.

Assess

Assess the external context, internal controls, and ethical culture.

Accurately calibrate what needs to be:
1. Controlled
2. Mitigated
3. Avoided
4. Transferred

Shrink the risk universe to something more manageable.

ethicsinsight.co

Build

Build a fit-for-purpose and right-sized framework.

Develop content, communications, training, and frameworks that are:
1. Straightforward
2. Intuitive
3. Engaging
4. Focused on outcomes and behaviours

Change

Change the way you approach and see risk – from blocker to enabler.

Iterate and adapt the previous steps to encourage risk:
1. Recognition
2. Discussion
3. Ownership
4. Adaptation

Help colleagues make better decisions.

ethicsinsight

Figure 8.1 Assess, build, and change: make risk relevant.

Successful Assessments

Risk is dynamic. New threats emerge, regulations develop, and your activities change. In the assessment phase, we keep abreast of external developments, (re)calibrate internal controls accordingly, and continuously check in with our people. Culture eats controls. If you remember, we need to understand if people understand, can access and trust our risk management frameworks, leadership, and culture. Do we walk our talk? With a sound and rounded assessment, we can shrink the risk universe to something more manageable and make decisions – in line with our values and appetite – about what to control, mitigate, avoid, or transfer.

- **Control** risks where you have considerable influence. For instance, access controls for electronic devices to reduce cyber threats.

- **Mitigation** usually flows from residual risks (those you just have to live with). A blend of training, disclosure requirements, and monitoring might help reduce your exposure to conflicts of interest, but they will likely remain.

- **Avoidance** is a surprisingly impactful strategy if you think laterally and build in delays. For example, when a client faced repeated corrupt extortion requests in a regional Indonesian city, they moved all licence and visa applications to Jakarta, where the risk was lower.

- **Transferring** risk is not just about insurance. It is not about kicking things down your supply chain to smaller (and less risk-mature organisations); it can be about collective action and leverage. If you're managing an infrastructure project and local authorities are playing corruption games with zoning and licensing, kick the problem up to the governor or the federal level. They need to get the project done, so make their bureaucrats' corrupt requests their problem.

Other strategies here include finding alternative ways to incentivise recalcitrant stakeholders. But, for starters, these tactics should get you going.

Building Design

With a defined and manageable risk map, we can build great content. But how? I like design thinking, which is just a fancy term to make us consider:

1. **What** do people need to know to do their work safely and ethically? Don't start with what the regulators want. They are not your audience if you want to manage risk.

2. **How** should we define the core concepts? Reduce your initial content (word count, training length, etc.) as much as possible.

3. **Why** does this matter to the users? Build a prototype, and get feedback from your users.

4. **Who** needs to know, and how do we relate to them? Stories will often help, especially those from within.

This process is how people build products, services, and content we like. I am far from a master in these arts and enjoy working with design-minded people. But I hope you will agree that some of the figures used in the book make concepts more accessible than long policies. For us in integrity risk, the bar is low. It's pretty easy to exceed user expectations when a 50-page code of conduct is heralded as transformative by industry peers because it uses a few cartoons and bright colours.

If we're trying to educate, inform, and empower people, we need to learn about learning. I talked about how little utility we derive from *one-and-done* training – annual borefests to tick a box. Without spaced repetition, we forget. Google Herman Ebbinghaus, and you'll soon find a model called The Forgetting Curve. If you don't remind us of a concept after the first impression, we forget. I am not suggesting you spam people with the same training every three days for a week or two. We all now have access to technologies that allow us to assess user responses and follow up accordingly. Refresh users on the content they get wrong repeatedly, basics! I can direct you if you need recommendations and further details about micro-learning. We waste so much time and money (opportunity cost) on the false economy that is your *one-and-done* training.

Finally, if you want to embed learning, provide cheat sheets, check-lists, and other visuals as takeaways. Training and communication are more about the latter than the former, yet we (typically) spend little effort on effective communications. We don't learn from didactic lectures and reading. We learn by doing. Give people the tools to practise the learning. You won't regret it.

Change Is Ethical Decision-Making

You're winning if you've accurately assessed your risk world and built content that resonates. As you finesse your training and communication, people will move up the knowledge curve, where they will demand more than *what* (not) to do, asking *how* to do it. We must provide our colleagues with risk assessment, identification, and ownership tools to facilitate this mastery.

I discussed my problem with many existing frameworks – the "is it legal and in line with our values?" steps. We need proactive and reactive models. Prevention is better than cure, but how? We need to teach our colleagues how to assess risk *before* action. Figure 8.2 summarises one such approach. The more we embed risk in (strategic) decisions, the fewer issues we will face. Planning prevents poor performance. When your colleagues (senior leaders in particular) start thinking like this, we change the culture and make risk relevant.

Issues happen, and things will go wrong. Sometimes external events – from war to pandemics – shake our foundations. In other cases, human error, malfeasance, or lousy luck knock us off course. The trick (a hard one) is not to panic. Systems and frameworks help. They're nothing without practice. Decision-making is a muscle requiring training. Crisis simulations can be a fantastic

Risk Assessment 101

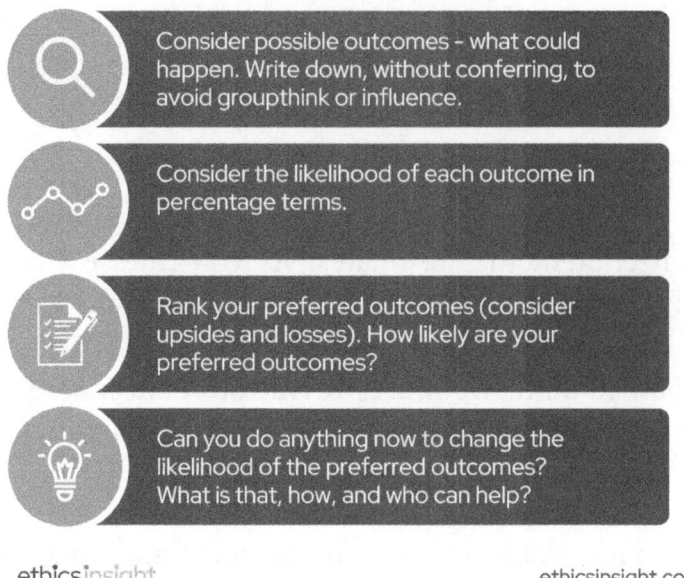

Consider possible outcomes - what could happen. Write down, without conferring, to avoid groupthink or influence.

Consider the likelihood of each outcome in percentage terms.

Rank your preferred outcomes (consider upsides and losses). How likely are your preferred outcomes?

Can you do anything now to change the likelihood of the preferred outcomes? What is that, how, and who can help?

ethicsinsight   ethicsinsight.co

Figure 8.2   Risk assessment 101.

sandbox to test out our ethics muscles. I like this model, as you'll have guessed by now:

1. What are the facts?

2. Don't make decisions based on assumptions; test what you can.

3. Rank scenarios by probability (in percentage terms).

4. Who do we need to inform, and who can help?

One proactive and one reactive assessment framework will be enough to navigate away from the more explosive ethical mine-fields. Train, test, and tweak. I've led leadership teams through

KEEPING IT SIMPLE AND COST-EFFECTIVE

desktop crisis simulations which went very badly – murdering local communities. Catastrophic. Not only does this provide a sobering reality check and plenty of learning, but it's also quite exhilarating. I'm not making light of serious issues. Failing in a safe space can be cathartic and infinitely preferable to the alternative. Furthermore, we like being tested. Fail in practice to succeed in reality.

The ABC process will right-size risk, which reduces costs.

Working on a Budget

As someone who has bootstrapped an advisory and SaaS business, budgets are my jam, and I have made a few suggestions that I hope might help.

Crown Jewels and Hacking Risk Assessments

A friend runs a remote-enabled microlearning platform based in Australia. Their clients are predominantly domestic private enterprises. So I was a little surprised when he messaged asking about an anti-corruption framework. I wondered why, as most of their business is subscription-based and transacted remotely – the face-to-face customer liaison is light, and governmental interactions are negligible. He replied, "The bank told us we need it." Large organisations love floating directionless directives downstream.

Most of you will receive such requests (especially if you're an SME). My advice to my friend was simple: "I'll send you some boilerplate policies to satisfy the demand, but what are you doing to protect your crown jewels?" Perplexed, we discussed how their organisation holds hundreds of thousands of people's data and is web-based. Information security and data privacy would seem bigger beasts. Start by protecting your crown jewels. What makes you, you? What can you not survive without?

If you don't know where to start, we offer free (or nearly free) options as part of our mission to democratise access to proper integrity risk assessment support. With greater clarity around (potential) gaps, it becomes much more cost-effective to plug them. If you're struggling, head to the Ethics Insight site or get in touch.

Crowdsource or Outsource?

There's very little that hasn't been done. Luckily, in my experience, the risk community is a sharing place. If you make an effort to contribute to the various industry associations and more informal groups, you'll receive humbling help. Ask people further down the path for assistance. You can also use LinkedIn, as I did, to crowdsource and finesse ideas – especially content we were building. A number of the figures in this book came via that channel.

Or you could outsource. That can work well if you have an advisor you trust, who gets you. But be careful if you're outsourcing without (proper) understanding. I've had some awful experiences, and the cost isn't always a reliable indicator. For instance, I needed help with some graphic templates when we updated the brand. The first provider received rave reviews and delivered a late, limp, and lifeless disaster. Someone half the price fixed the mess. I have to own my part. I learned from failure. It sharpened my understanding of what I *didn't* want. Be clear in your instruction and intention if you're getting external support. If you need legal advisors, choose ones who have seen frontline risk – there is an inverse correlation between glitzy offices and practicable advice.

Make It Their Job

If you have the leadership buy-in, risk management could be part of people's incentives and KPIs. Radical, I know. Yes, they will need support, but I've observed a paradox with risk – the more internal resources (people), the less people think. If colleagues know there is a (large) risk or compliance team, there can be a tendency to abdicate personal responsibility. Best case, they'll pass on every knotty (or not) problem to you. Worst case, they'll comply. We started in the Introduction with the example of bankers taking a rigid approach to compliance – *if we didn't catch them murdering, it's legal.* Some of the most tightly regulated sectors create the largest scandals. The briefest glance at fines for corruption, money laundering, and other violations bears this out. More rules – plus terrible incentive cultures – create fools.

If you have the luxury of (something of) a clean slate, use it. Set realistic rewards, KPIs, and goals. Make your colleagues own risks relevant to their areas of operation and expertise. Help, counsel, and guide, but don't smother or spoil them. Make risk relevant to them.

INDEX